NIGHT OF THE LIVING DEAD '90

THE VERSION YOU'VE NEVER SEEN

By Tom Savini

Happy Cloud Media, LLC
www.happycloudpictures.net

ACKNOWLEDGEMENTS

*The Publishers would like to thank the following for their
invaluable contributions, support, and all-around well-wishing:
Brad Hunter, Christine Forest, Jason Baker, Dave Dreher, Michael Felsher, Christian Stavrakis,
Phillip R. Rogers, Ken and Pam Kish and Cinema Wasteland, Amy Lynn Best,
Patricia Tallman, Bill Moseley, William Butler, Terry Thome, and
Jonas Barbosa and the Official Night of the Living Dead (1990) Facebook Group.*

NOTE: All text written by Tom Savini. Quotes from Bill Moseley and Patricia Tallman come from interviews conducted between 2002 and 2003 by editor Mike Watt.

Storyboard art by Brad Hunter

Cover art by Christian Stavrakis

Layout and Design by Ryan Hose

**NIGHT OF THE LIVING DEAD 1990: THE VERSION YOU'VE NEVER SEEN
By Tom Savini © 2019 Happy Cloud Media, LLC**

Photos and storyboards come from the personal collection of Tom Savini.

ISBN-13: 978-1-951036-15-7
BISAC: Performing Arts / Film & Video / History & Criticism

No part of this book may be reproduced or transmitted in any form or by any means, electronic or mechanical, including photocopying or recording, or by any information storage and retrieval system, without permission in writing from the publisher.

Happy Cloud Media, LLC is owned and operated by Amy Lynn Best and Mike Watt.
www.happycloudpictures.net

NIGHT OF THE LIVING DEAD '90

THE VERSION YOU'VE NEVER SEEN

The wall in my office with all the boards.

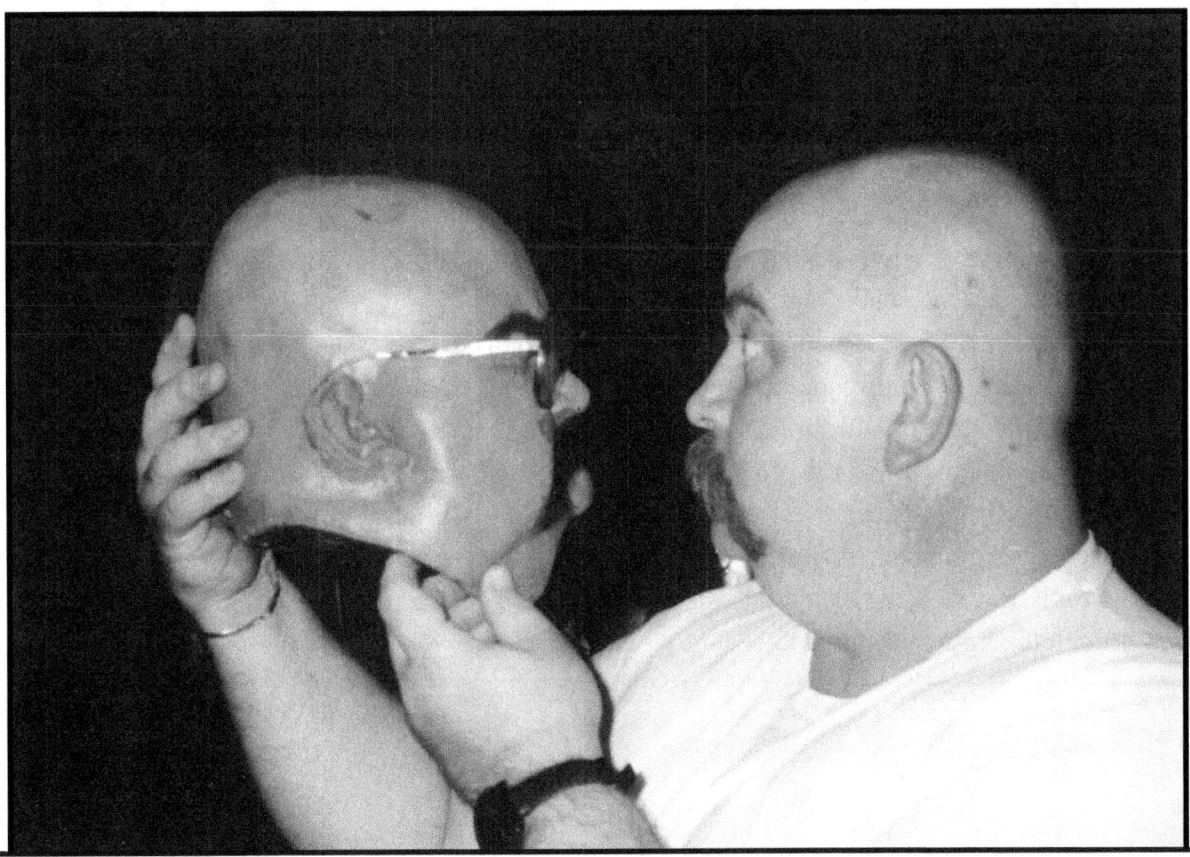

Pat Logan (Uncle Reege) contemplates his head.

"I was just so happy to get the job and be working with Tom Savini again. He sent me a copy of the script and said 'Pick any character that you want'. I went through and started picking characters, the Tommy Toles character the Billy Butler character, ones that had more scenes. [Laughs] And he called me back and said 'Sorry, I meant, pick any character, just make sure it's Johnny'.

It was nice to actually just be a human being for a change. And a victim. John Vulich and Everette Burrell made that nice dummy for me. Which my merciful stand-in for the head-against-the-tombstone gag. There was a debate whether to use a dummy and a real tombstone, or to use me and a fake tombstone. And I think the shot itself is just awesome. It's just so powerful. And also, wrestling with the zombie, that was pretty much unchoreographed. We did a tiny bit of choreography, but Tom just wanted us to go for it. It was a little dangerous, since we were surrounded by marble tombstones. But I think the fight looks great too."

— Bill Moseley

"I like the fact that Barbara was this little school teacher person. A normal little lady who was probably very unused to standing up for herself at all until this happened. I like that I got the chance to make that transformation, where she goes from being a normal person. And maybe the fans could get the feeling that that could be anybody—that could be them! You never know how brave you can be. You may not think you're a brave person, but if you're pushed up against the wall, you would do what you could! And everyone likes to think they would, right? So that was a pleasure in being her. She didn't start off being Red Sonja. She was a normal lady in an extraordinary circumstance."

—Patricia Tallman

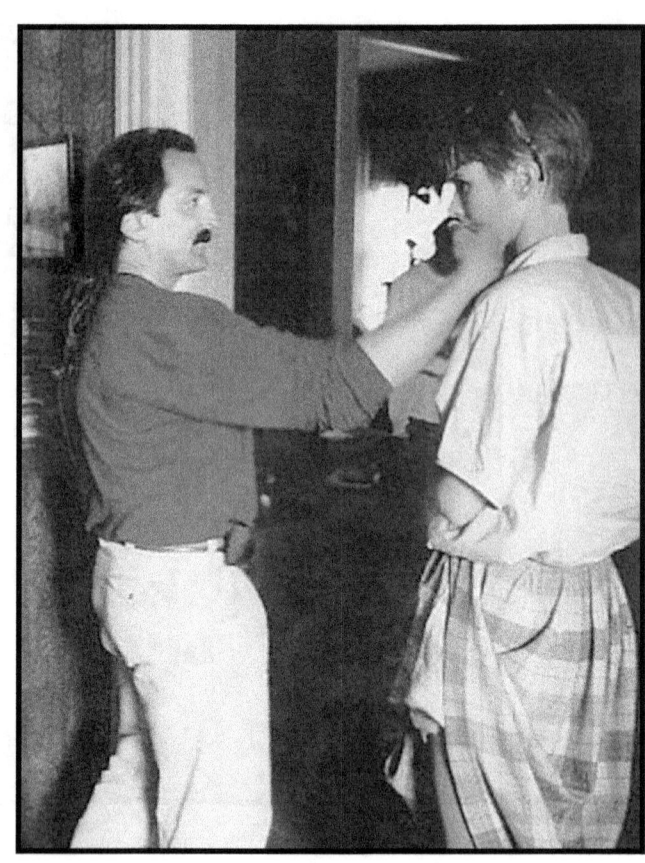
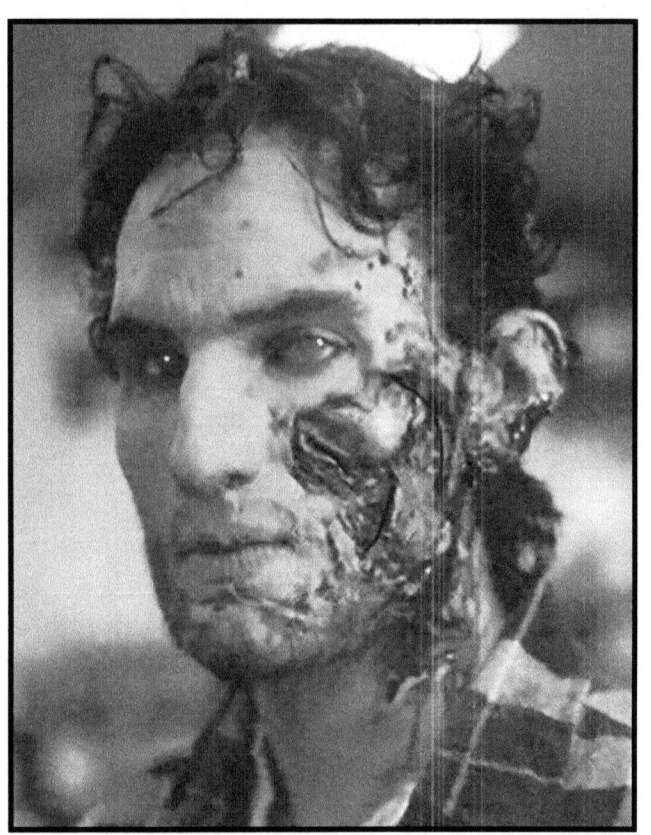
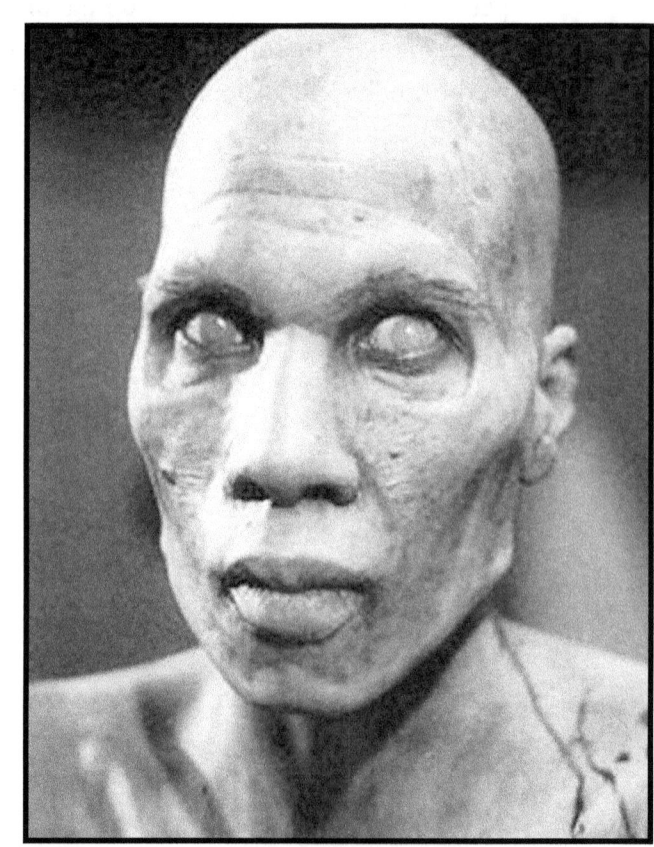

INTRODUCTION BY TOM SAVINI

So I'm walking with George Romero somewhere and he turns to me and says, "I just got financing to remake *Night of the Living Dead*."

I thought, "Holy shit." Having created the make up effects on most of his pictures up to that time, I now get to make zombies again for a George Romero picture. Then he says, looking me right in the eyes: "I want *you* to direct it."

'*Boing*' went the cartoon sound effect in my head. I was gobsmacked and thanked the hell out of him. There was some time before we were scheduled to start shooting so the first thing I did was call Brad Hunter and we worked together creating these storyboards. I wanted to shoot the whole movie on paper first. That's what Hitchcock and many other directors did. I think I read Hitchcock hated shooting the movie because he already made the movie when he created it on paper.

I put the boards in order on the wall of my office so when anyone came in, like the set designer, or costumes, or anyone connected with the picture, I could go from beginning to end and show them the movie I had planned. When George Romero came in and I ran through the boards, he said, "Those are great but you have a six-week movie up there and you only have four weeks to shoot it." So we started cutting stuff before we even began.

I refer to the cuts here as "THAT WAS SHOT DOWN."

Time was my biggest enemy on this production, and though everyone seems to love this picture, I didn't get to show you *The Version You've Never Seen*…until now.

George was there for the first one or two days of shooting in the cemetery, but had to leave for his home in Florida to write *The Dark Half*. He had a deadline. I heard him keep saying, "Tom doesn't want us here, we are making him nervous." And I exclaimed, "No! I love that you're here."

I really did love him being there. My whole motivation was to please him, to impress him. He wanted me to direct this thing because the three episodes of *Tales from the Darkside* that I directed impressed him. Two of my episodes were the only ones, out of seventy-four of them, that they commissioned feature-length scripts written to hopefully produce. It would have been a lot smoother if he had been there for the *NOTLD* shoot…and a lot more fun.

I refer in here to the sleazy scumbag of a producer who constantly lied to George over the phone about what was going on during the shoot. Just so you know, I am not referring to Jack Russo, or Russ Streiner, or Christine Romero. They were lovely and encouraging and we are good friends to this day. You figure it out.

Okay, here's the plan. My version of *Night of the Living Dead* was basically, originally, going to be the same as George's version for maybe the first half of the movie, with misdirections, using your knowledge of the original film to fool you and give me the opportunity for some jump scares. We call them CHAIR JUMPERS.

People have seen and have become so familiar with the original I wanted mine to be innovative and interesting and travel new ground. I wanted it to start in black-and-white, beginning with the studio logo. An homage to the original and a comfort-zone link between the two versions. It would start that way, and then slowly color would seep in for the rest of the movie. THAT WAS SHOT DOWN.

I also wanted a ZOMBIE POINT OF VIEW. A decrepid, black-and-white, in-and-out-of-focus footage that would be what a zombie is seeing. I could use this footage to build suspense. For example if you are looking at two people talking, or walking, or doing stuff like looking for keys in Uncle Rege's pocket, and suddenly I cut to the unusual black-and-white

established point-of-view of a zombie or zombies approaching…from that second on the suspense of you knowing the zombies are coming—but the characters don't—would exist. George said no, the zombies are dead and that might give life to them or something like that. I said, "Well, they aren't bumping into things like they are blind." But…THAT WAS SHOT DOWN.

So I said it would be basically the same for about the first half of the movie, and then you would start seeing some changes. Drastic changes from the original.

The Version You've Never Seen really begins with Barbara at the cemetery. Barbara, at the cemetery, isn't all there. I didn't want her to be the comatose brain dead twit in the original, beautifully played by my good friend and dancing partner Judy O'Dea. I wanted to film something that was going on in her mind from the first shots in the cemetery, as she looks at the graves of children and family members. She was still mourning her mother and hearing her voice…as well as the voices of the names she was seeing on the gravestones. THAT WAS SHOT DOWN.

I wanted Barbara to come back at the end and help fight the zombies. George said she is dead, and I reminded him that we don't see her killed in his version. 'She is merely dragged away. Why can't she get away and come back?' Well, certainly *that* Barbara, *his* Barbara, might not do that but I had my intention set that Barbara, *my* Barbara, would change into a ruthless fighter. A hero…Patty Tallman. The beginning of *The Version You've Never Seen*.

There is a reason that their mother's photo is on the tombstone, and how it plays an important part in Barbara's psyche, and why we had to cut it from the film. I've seen these photos on tombstones at the nearby Allegheny Cemetery—which, by the way, is where I wanted to shoot the beginning of my picture. It would have meant a long move from Washington, PA, where we did shoot, and it just wasn't practical. But it is a sprawling beautiful cemetery here in my neighborhood. Vast and hilly and would have been a whole different beginning. The cemetery we used did have the advantage of being able to see miles in the distance, and that Johnny and Barbara are in the middle of nowhere. You will see later why the mother's photo is on the tombstone…

The controversial "Mother-lookalike" zombie we couldn't use at the window.

THE STORYBOARDS

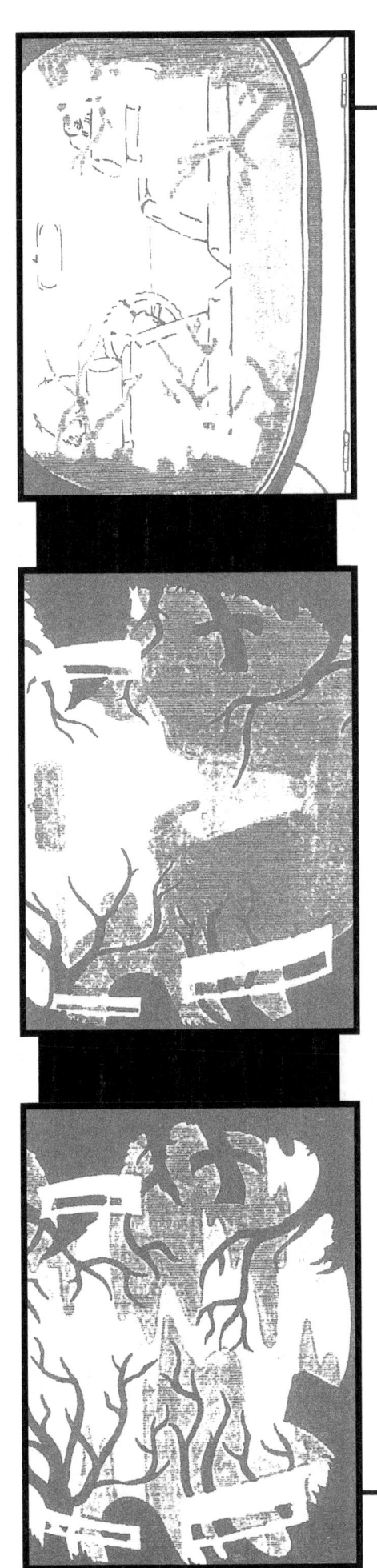

As I said, I wanted the film to be in black-and-white at the beginning and slowly transform into color. The very first images I wanted you to see were black and white shapes rising from the bottom of the frame ascending upwards for a bit. These images were actually reflections in the windshield of the car driven by Johnny with Barbara.

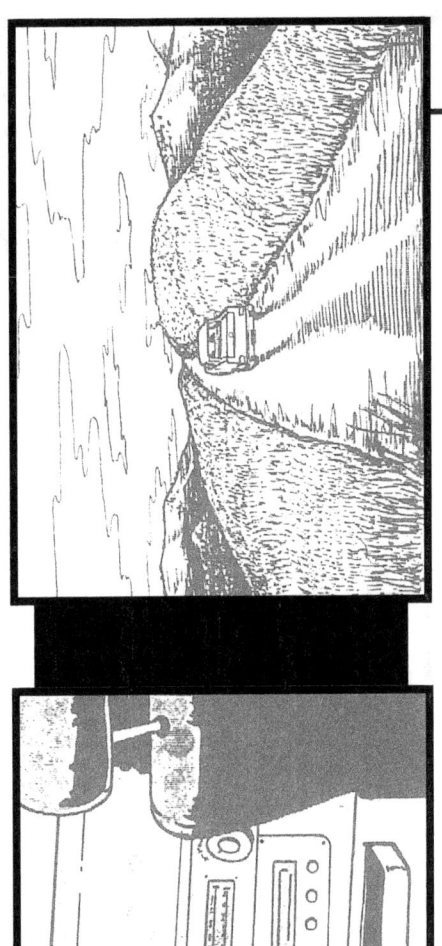

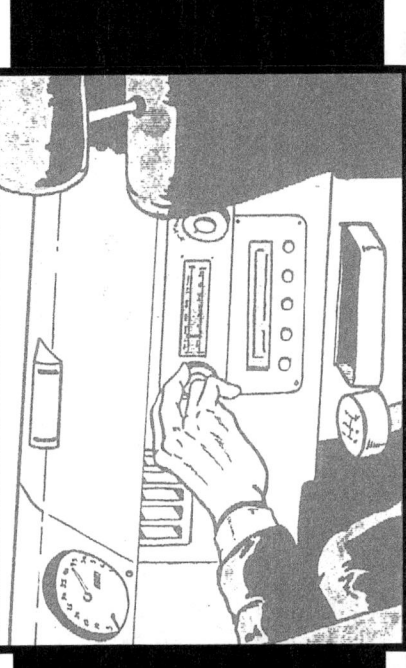

Eventually we are in the car with them and nothing is on the radio yet. I didn't want to see any sign of civilization close by or in the distance to give you the feeling that they are really in the middle of nowhere and that there would be no help close by.

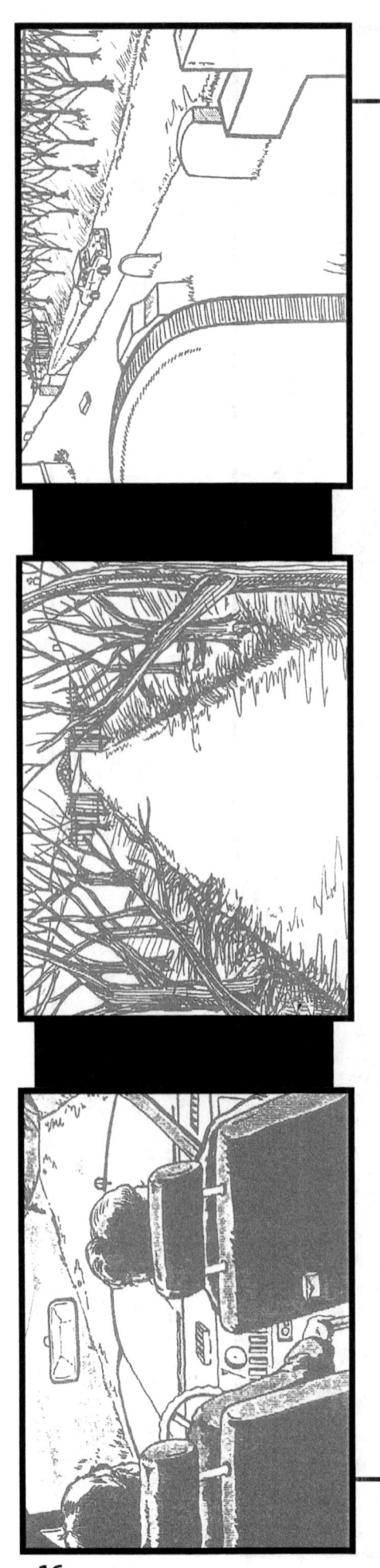

We start to hear Johnny's dialogue with Barbara, which is essentially the same as the original. All of this would still be in black and white...desolate...lonely.

As they approach the cemetery Johnny's dialogue continues, but soon he is drowned out by the voices in Barbara's head....

...But something changes. The mood inside the car: Johnny is bantering but Barbara is looking at the gravestones. We hear her thoughts; she attaches voices to the names on the graves. Slices of life. "Honey I'm home," or she sees a child's grave and hears children playing.

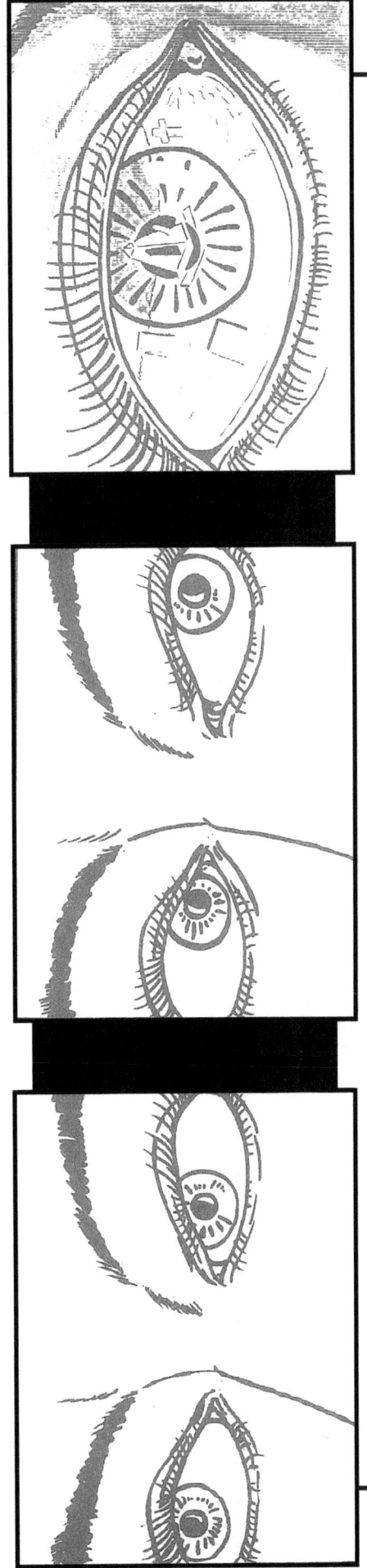

We are close on Barbara's eyes as we tune out Johnny and hear what she hears in her mind. All of this was to start building a persona of Barbara that is not-too-stable, and to re-establish what death is to her and to you the audience.

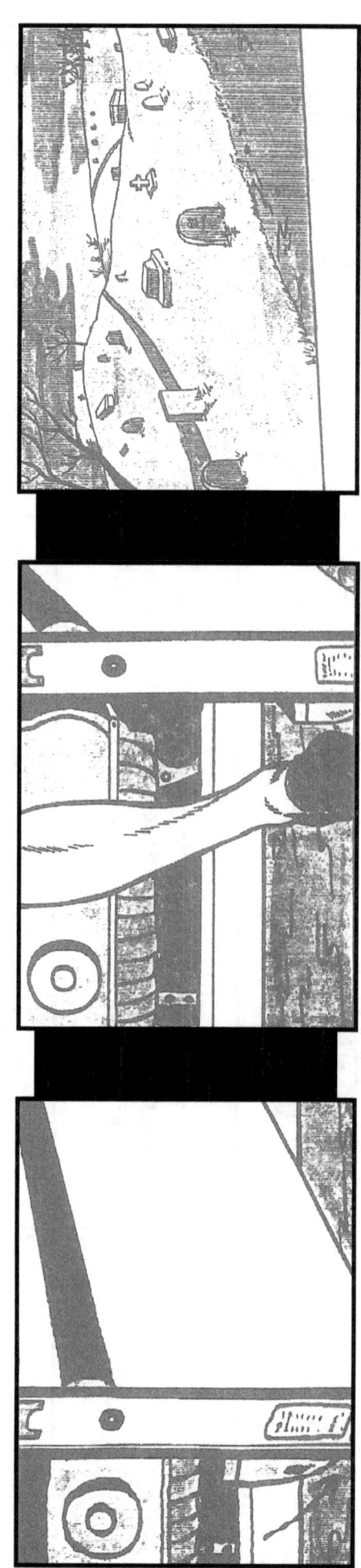

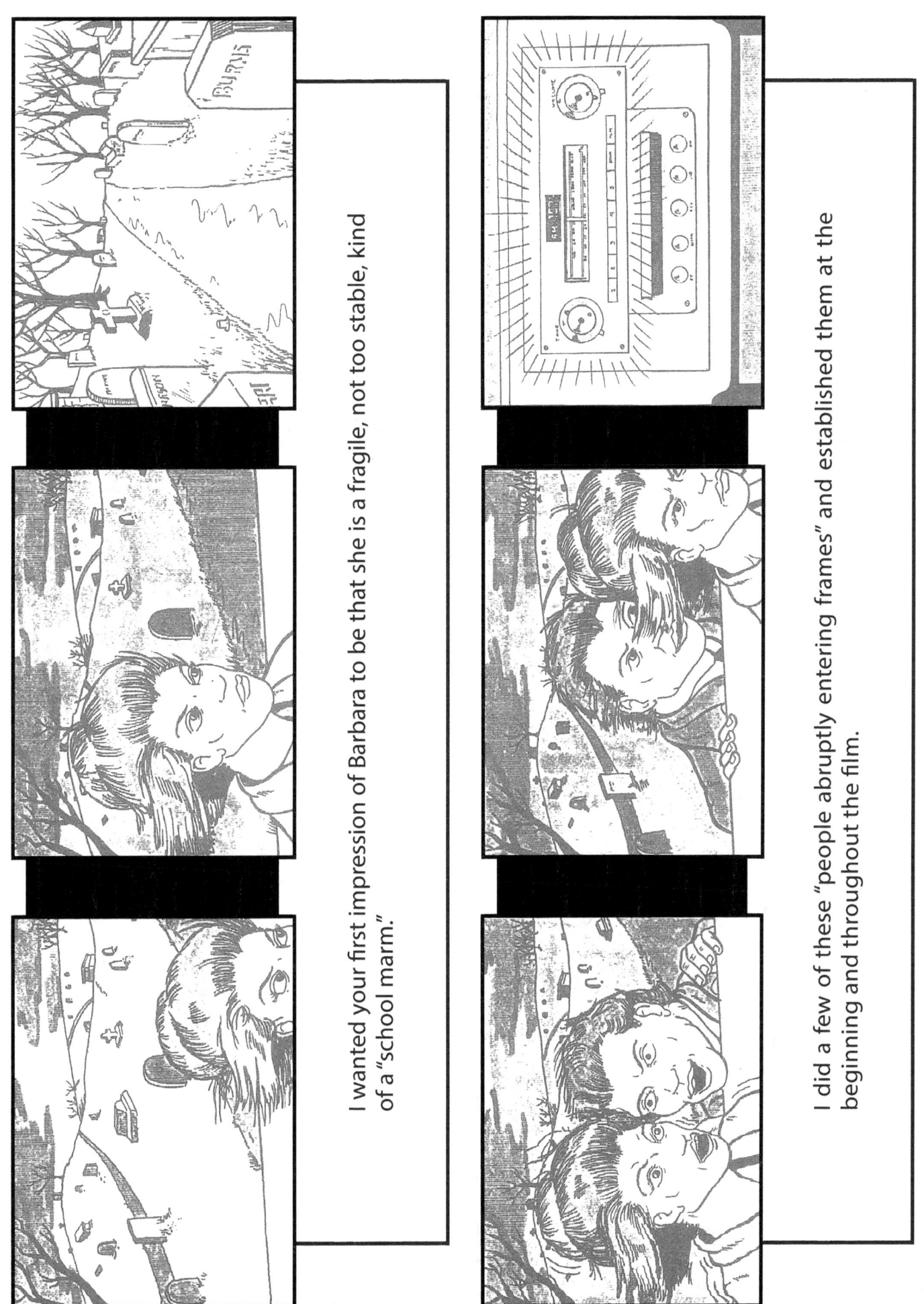

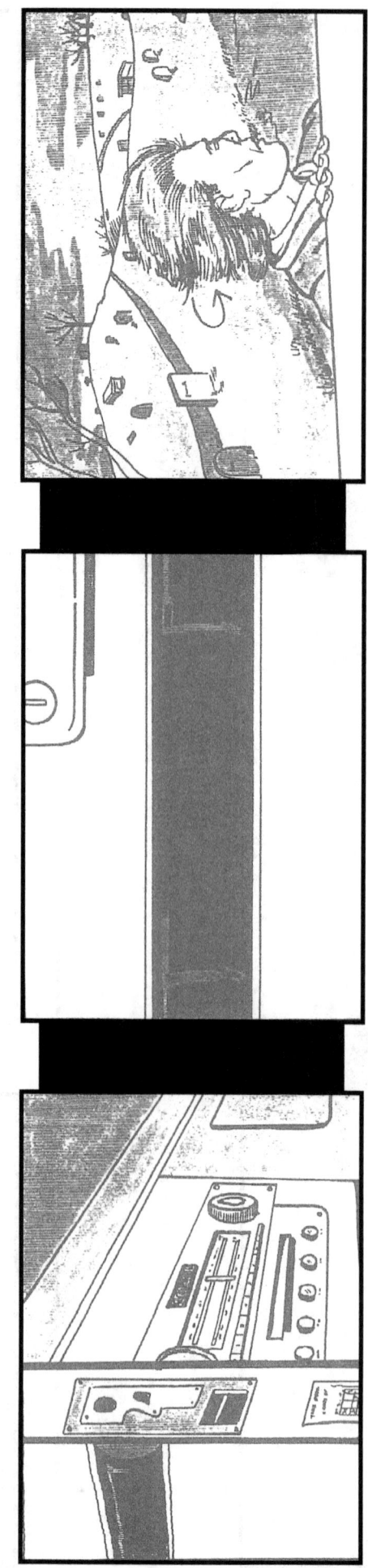

I really wanted you see what their mother looked like, because of a zombie apparition that takes place in Barbara's mind later. I even gave her a funny hat to stick in your memory.

I wanted to use your knowledge of the original to manipulate you…to scare you as in the case of the first person you see in the cemetery. In the original it is a zombie, so you expect this guy to be one. He is actually a mourner. My theatre friend, Pat Reese.

When he gets close to Johnny and Barbara you realize he is not a zombie and he apologizes to them and walks away, confused and lost. This would put you off guard and confuse you as well.

The whole idea was to manipulate you and misdirect you to follow Pat as he walked away.

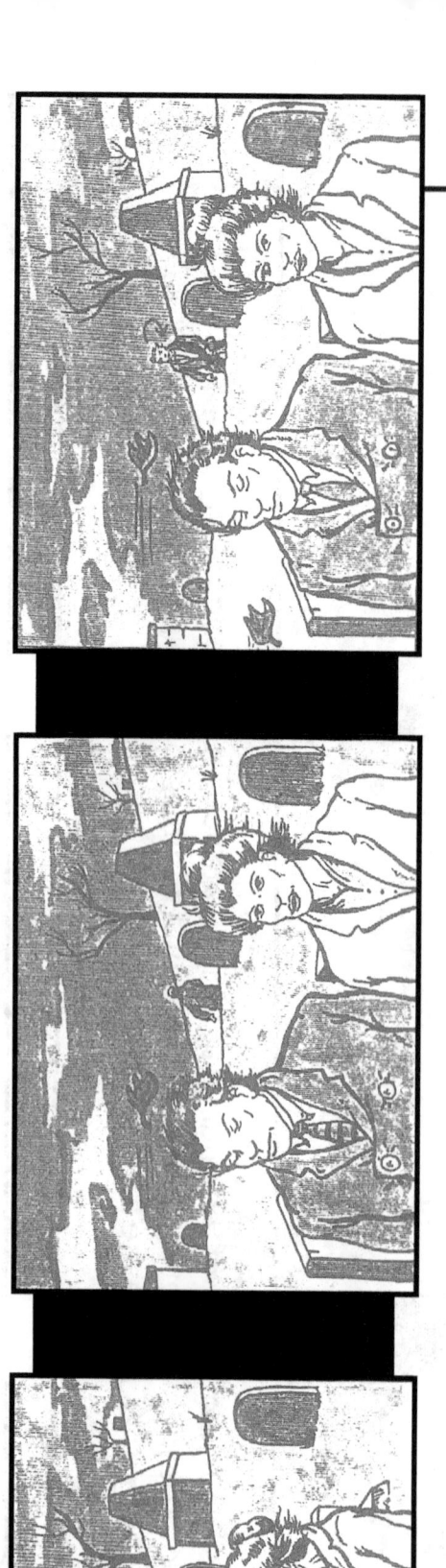

...And at the last minute have him turn to get your attention to him so that....

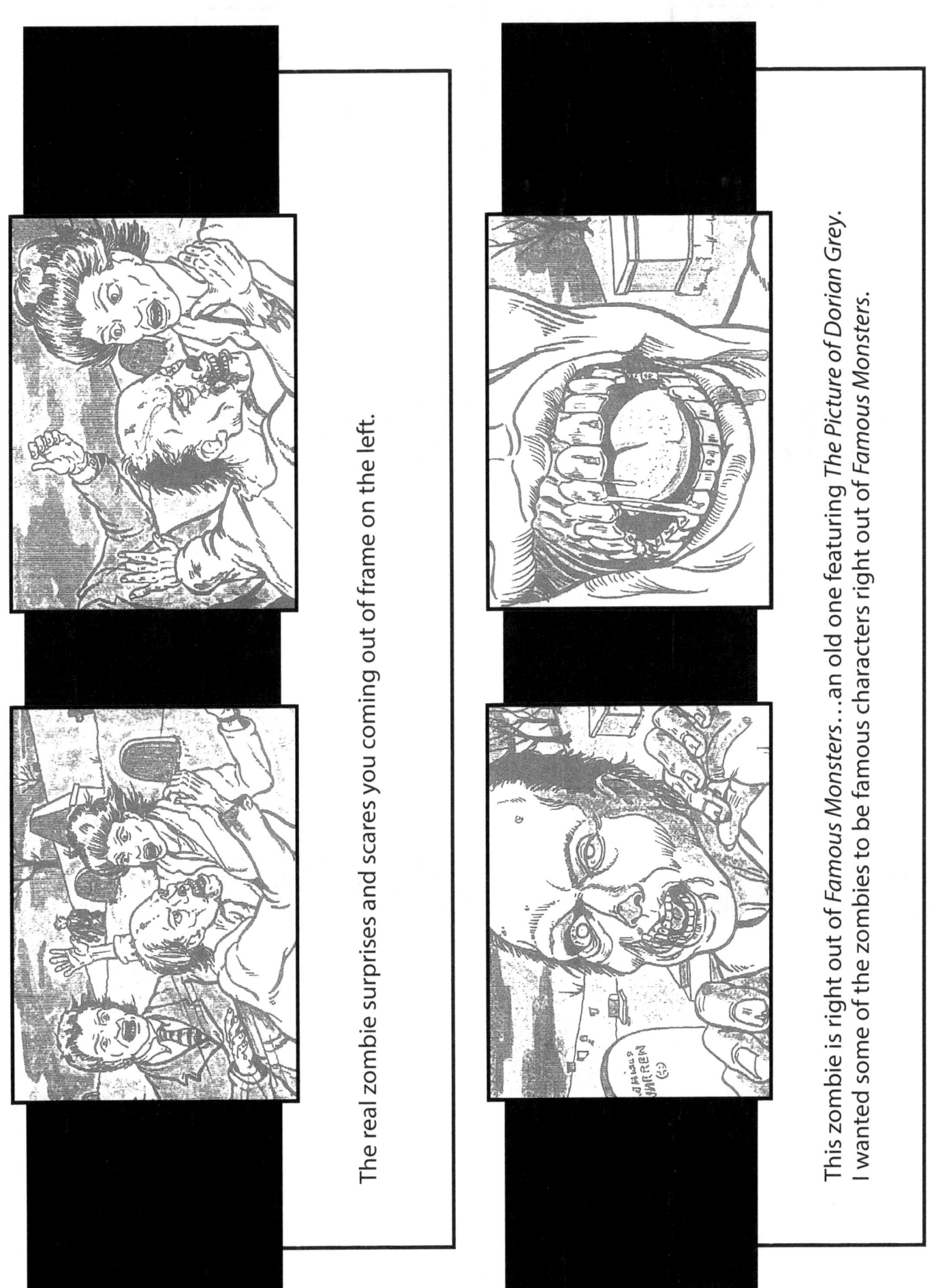

The real zombie surprises and scares you coming out of frame on the left.

This zombie is right out of Famous Monsters...an old one featuring The Picture of Dorian Grey. I wanted some of the zombies to be famous characters right out of Famous Monsters.

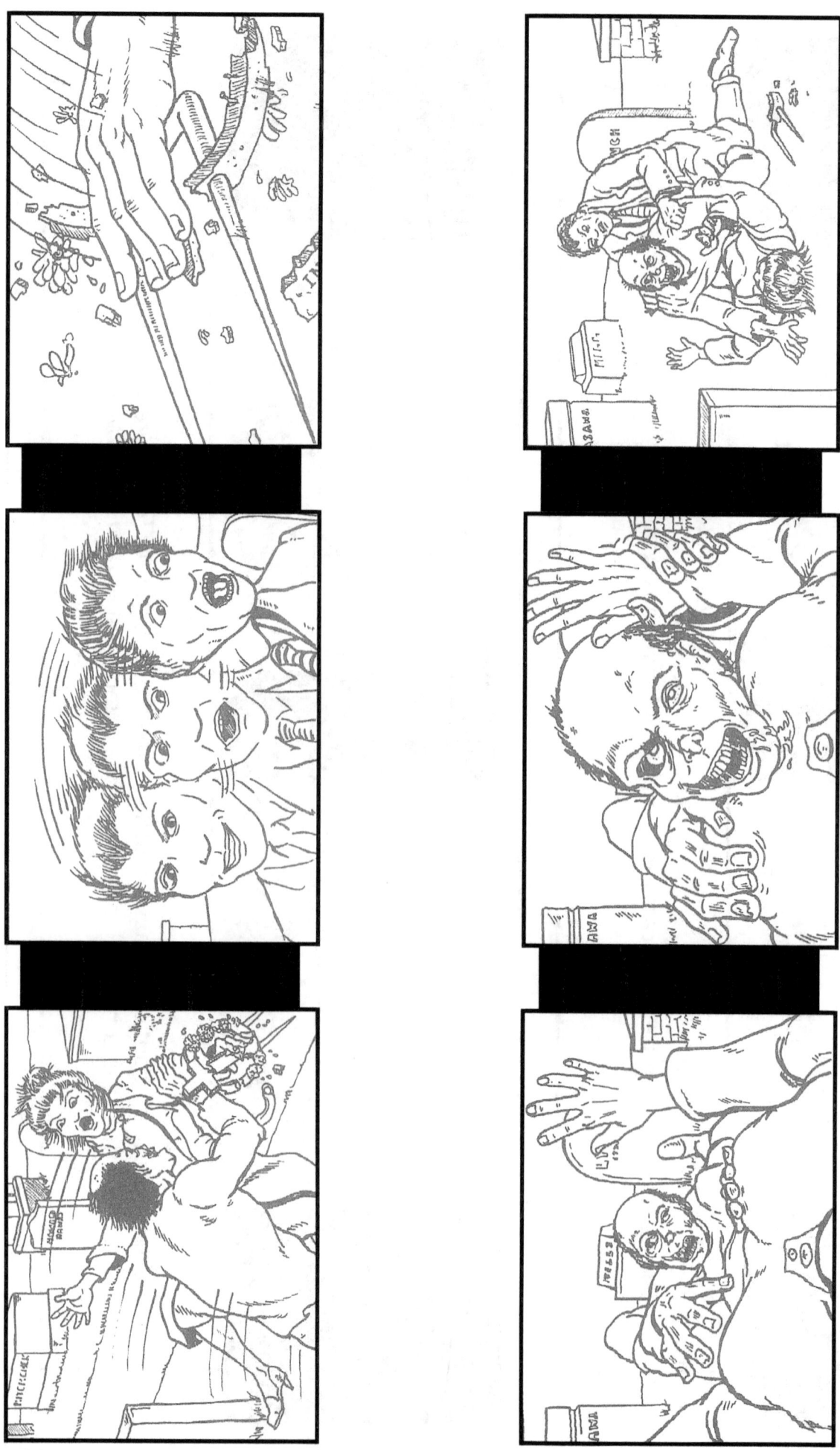

I wanted this to be a knock-down, dragged-out fight between Barbara and Johnny and the zombie. My effects guys built me a fake leg of Barbara so I could show it making contact with the zombies face. She had lost her shoe by then, so in the film that leg is barefoot.

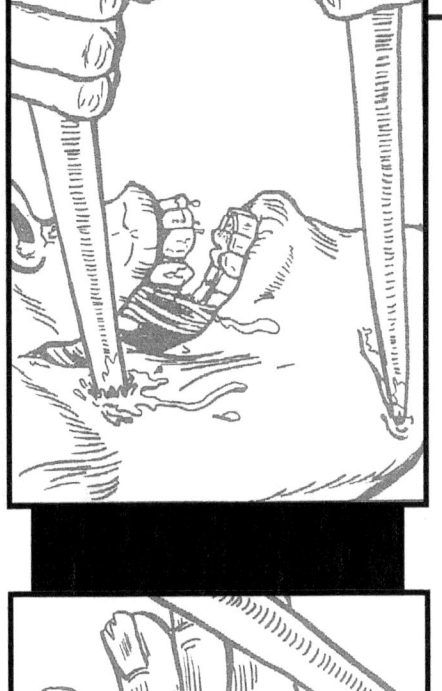

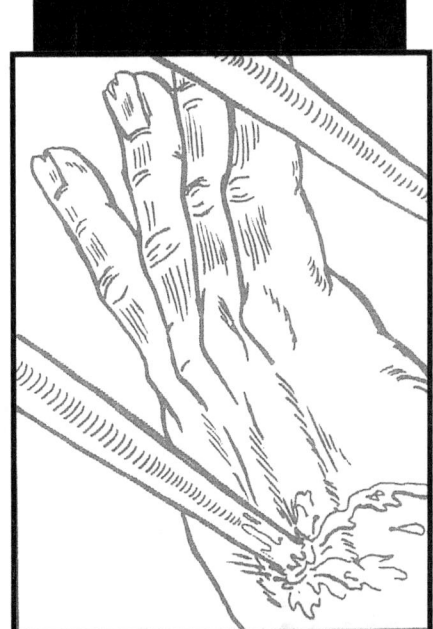

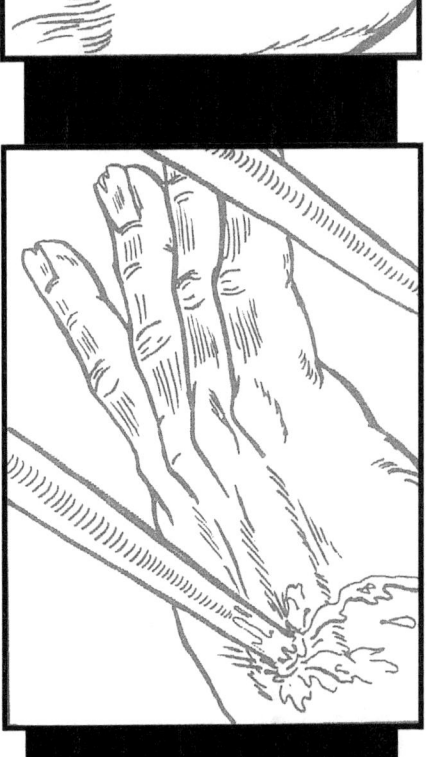

Also, we made retractable prongs on the flower arrangement that first strikes Johnny's hand in the confusion, and then is planted into the zombie, who continues to wear it when you see him toward the end when Barbara finally shoots him.

I specifically shot the zombies and Johnny's feet getting entangled during the fight so I could shoot them falling.

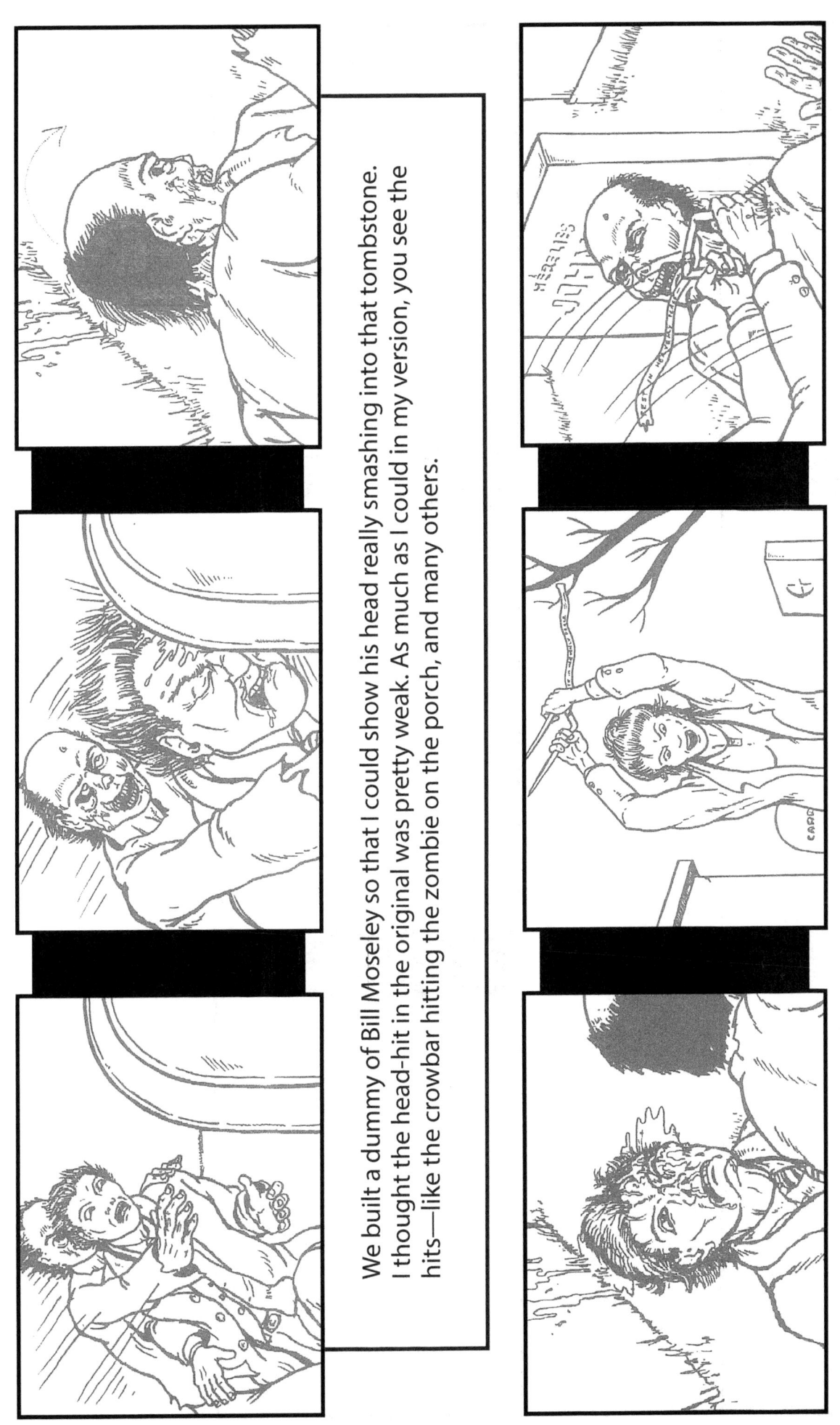

We built a dummy of Bill Moseley so that I could show his head really smashing into that tombstone. I thought the head-hit in the original was pretty weak. As much as I could in my version, you see the hits—like the crowbar hitting the zombie on the porch, and many others.

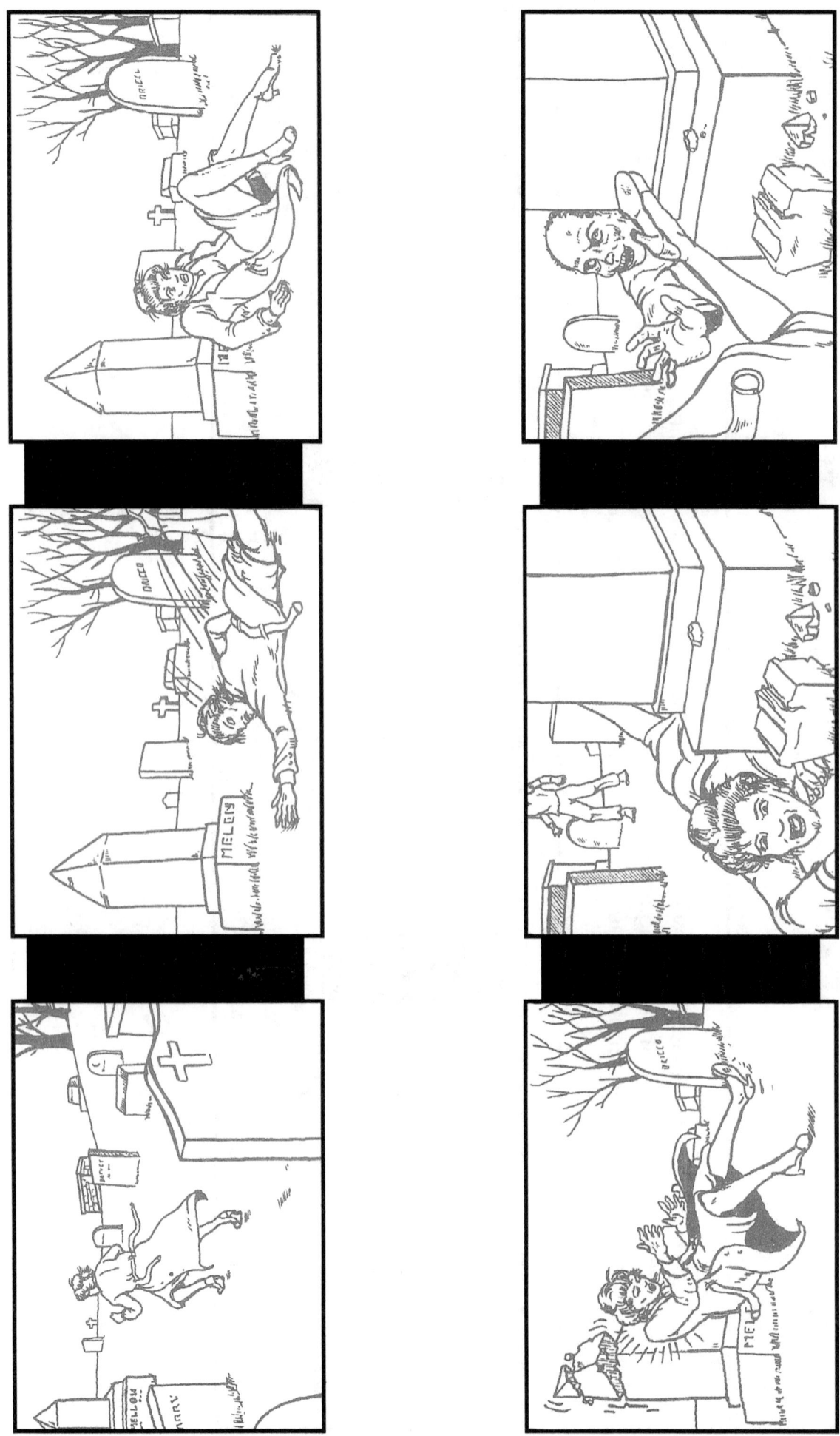

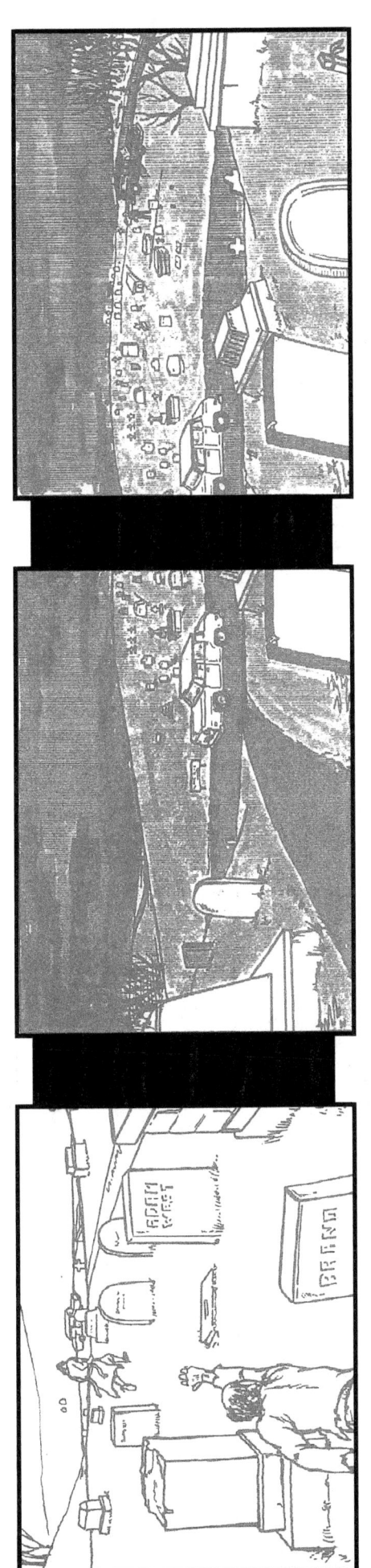

Another effect that was not in the script is the Funeral Home Zombie. We hint at it when we see the empty coffin and hearse. Barbara is really in the car when she sees him and thinks he is a normal human that could help her.

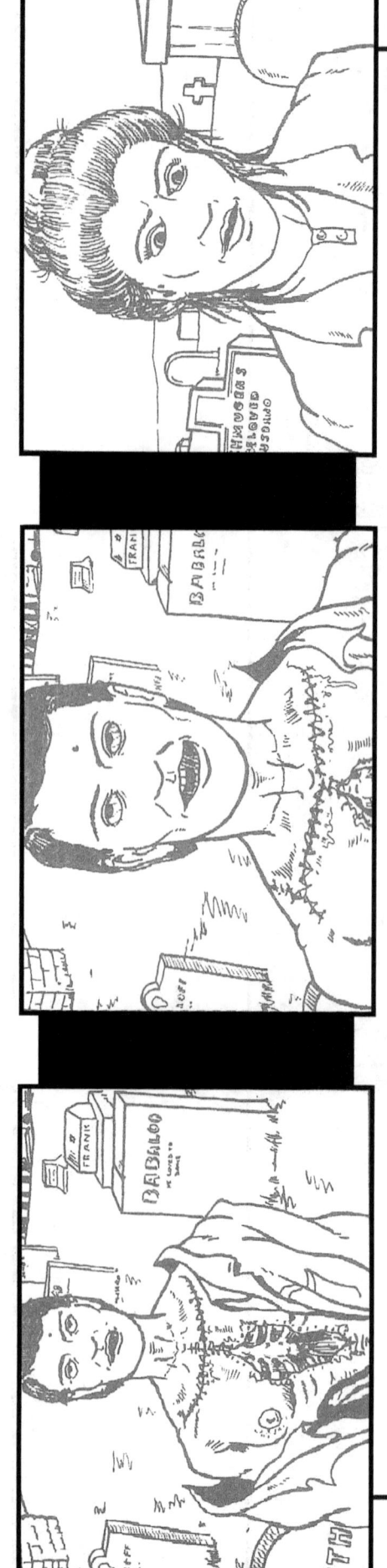

That day they were telling me we didn't have time to shoot The Autopsy Zombie, played by Tim Carrier stepping on his pants so that his autopsy stitching would be revealed. I had to insist and we got it shot. It's one of the great moments in the beginning action.

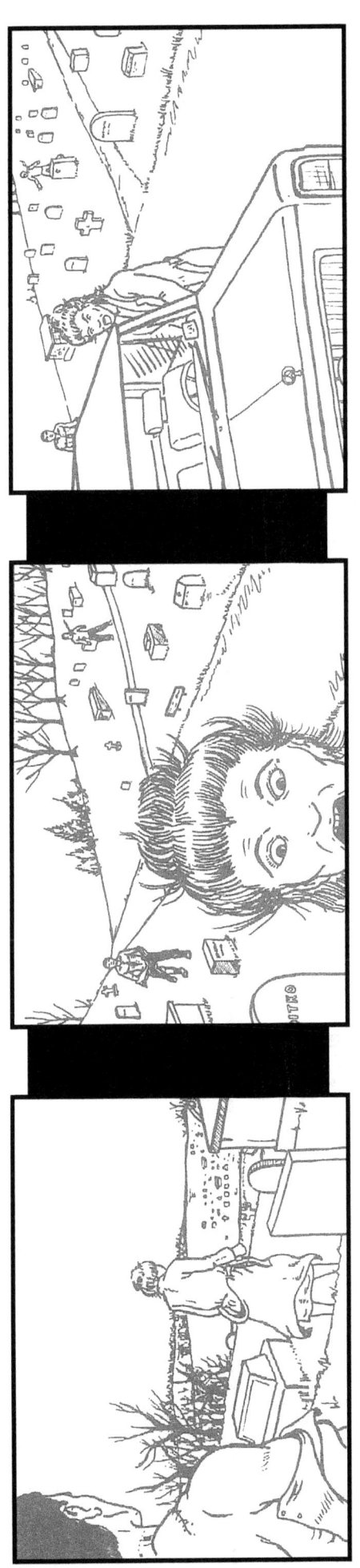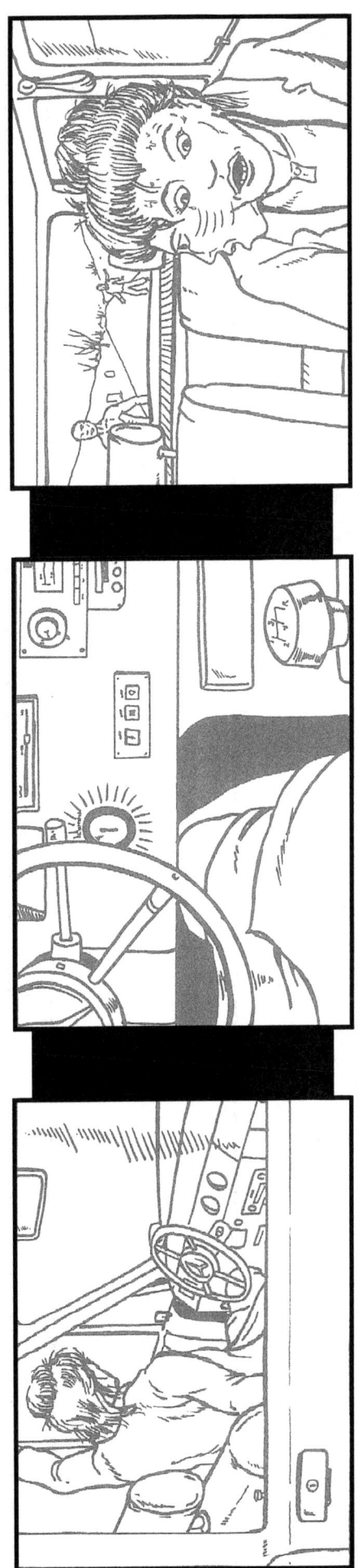

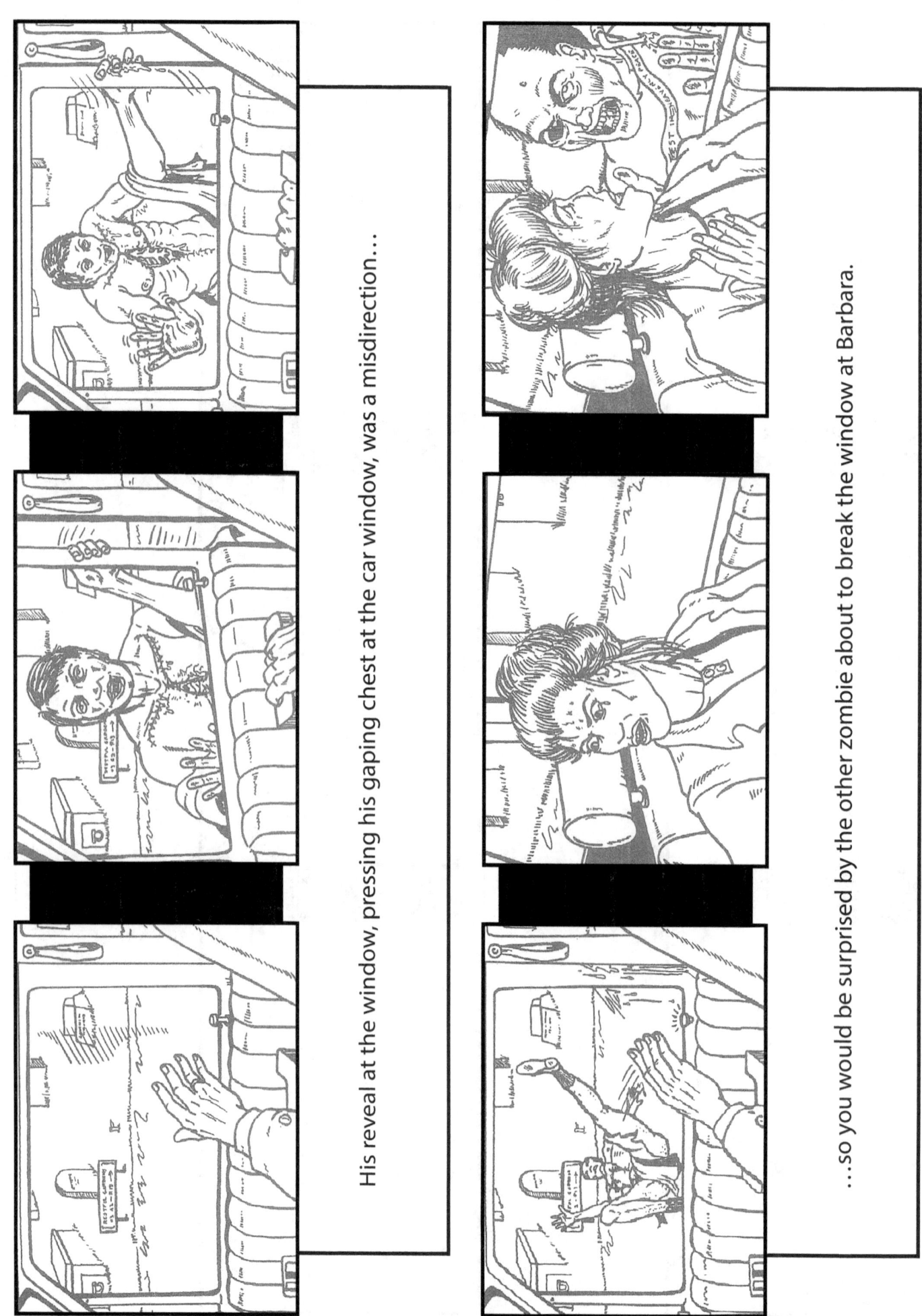

With zombies hanging onto the car it slides backwards toward the trees. I was hoping to run over a zombie or two. Time…you bastard.

She frantically looks in the glove compartment for the keys—but when the window breaks and he grabs her hair she can only think quick and pull the emergency brake.

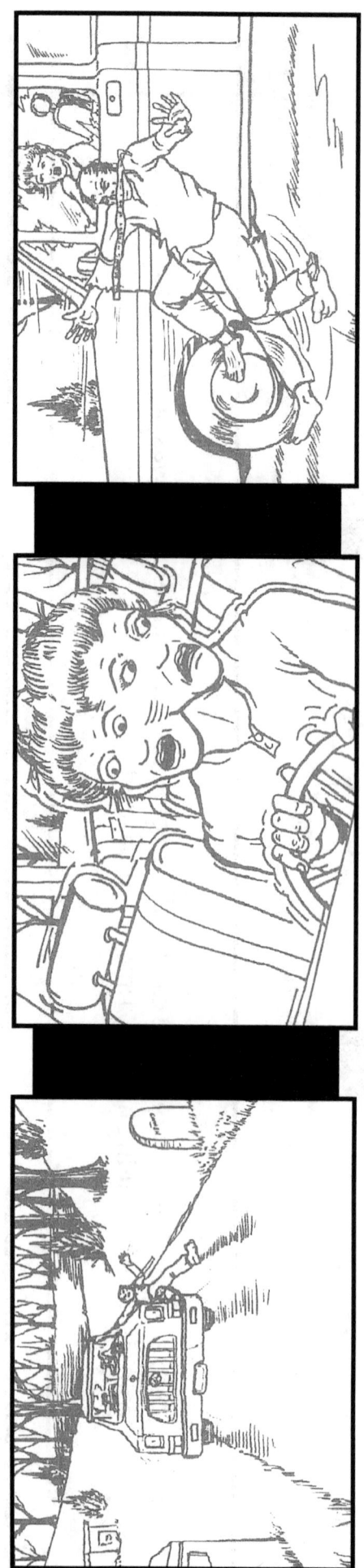

I wanted that car to really crash. In the original it kind of scraped a tree. In mine the whole backend is smashed in. The Mercedes was mine and I sold it to the company for these scenes. I should have sent the footage to Mercedes as it shows the crash did not invade the cabin but stopped short.

Barbara gets out of the car and barefoots it into the woods. She sees the farmhouse in the distance. If you look at the film you see Barbara yelling "Hello" into the barn. If you look at that scene you don't notice that somebody at floor level behind a barrel is slipping shoes onto her. I did that because the driveway leading to the house was gravel.

Only one reviewer of the many that reviewed the film caught on to why the nameplate on the house said "M.Celeste."

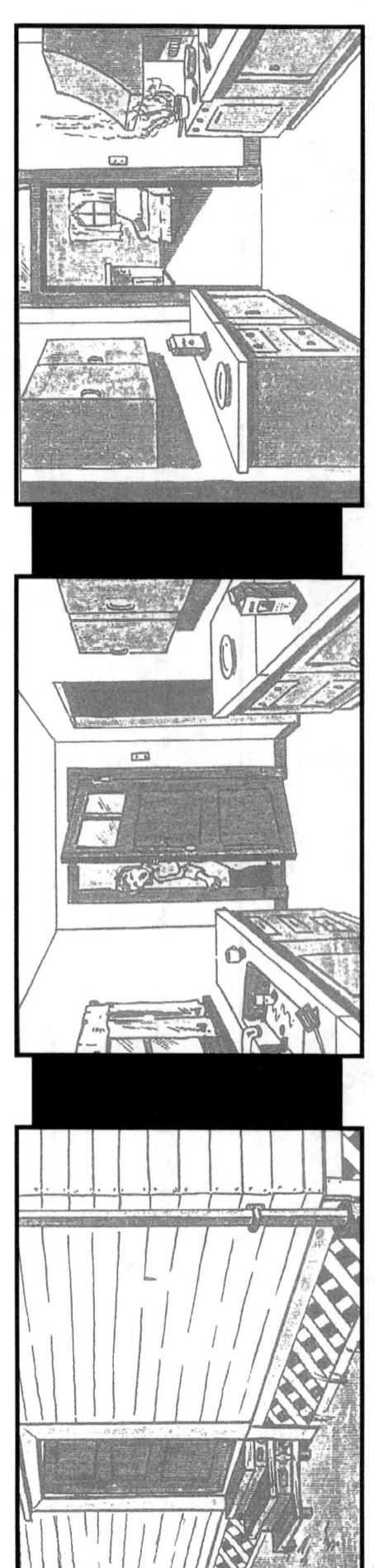
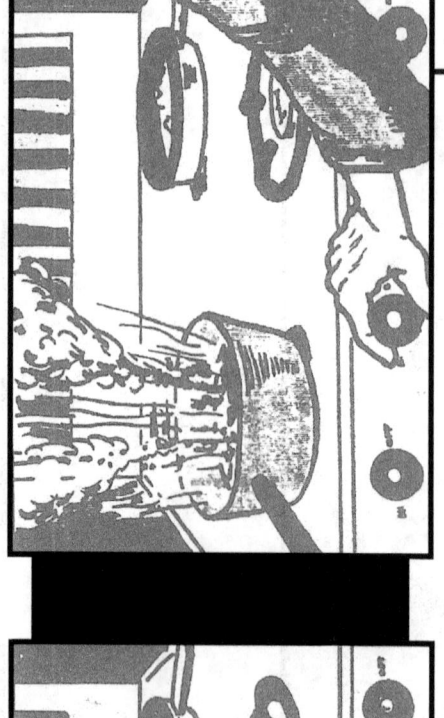
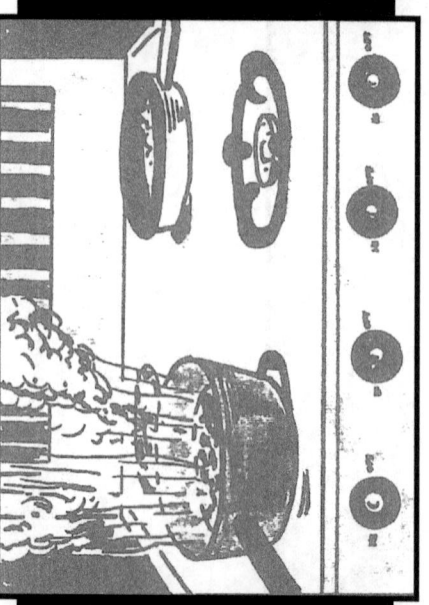
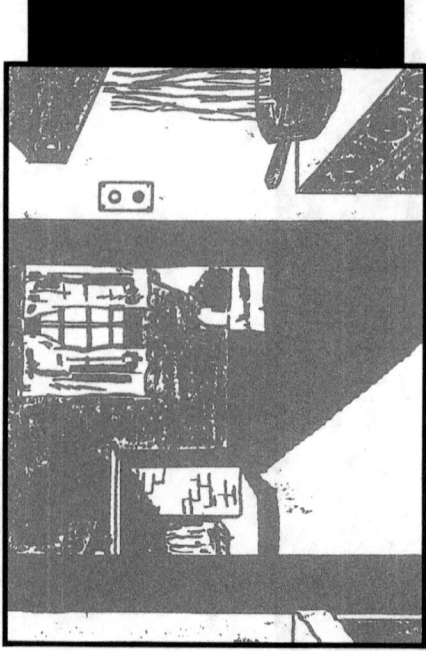

It has to do with the wreck of the "Mary Celeste," a boat found adrift in 1872 with no one aboard, yet food was cooking, there were cigars in the ashtrays, and clothes in the closets, but no one aboard. Kind of similar to what Barbara finds in the house. Get it?

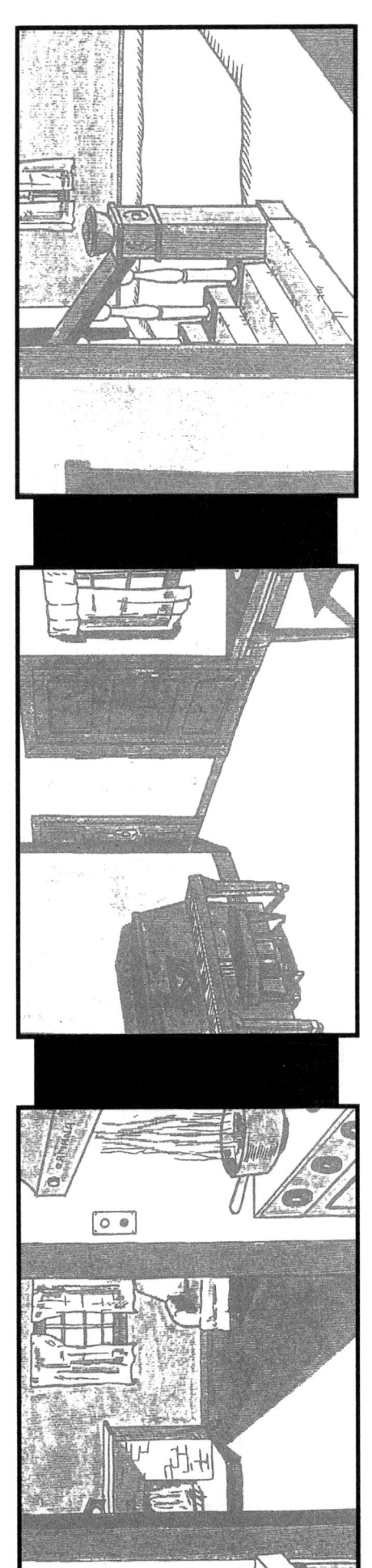
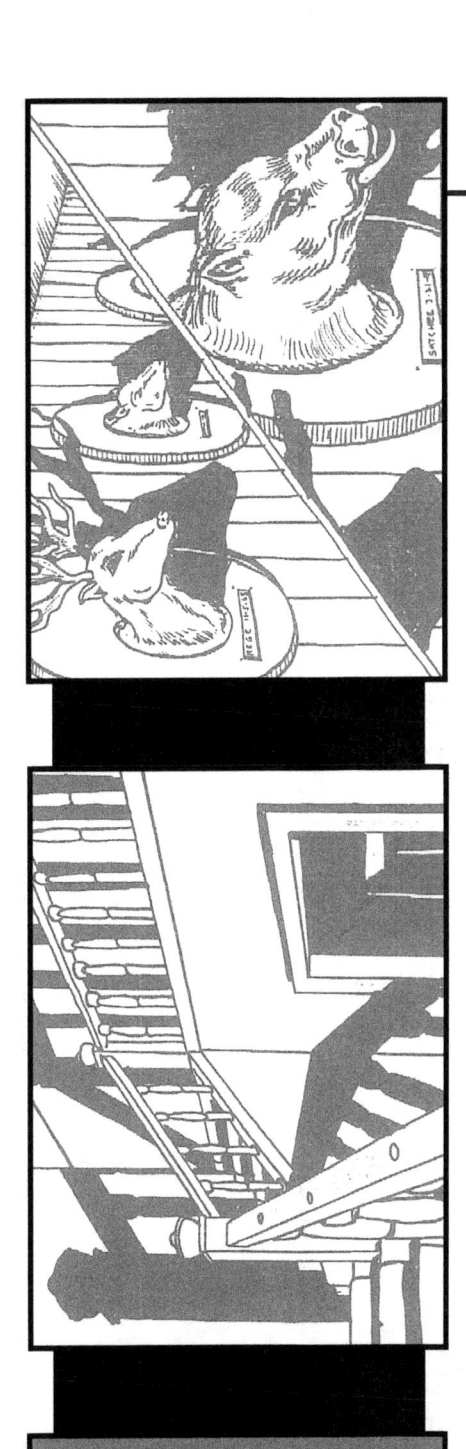

Barbara comes into the house calling, "Hello." Quiet. The animal trophies on the wall are an homage to George's version.

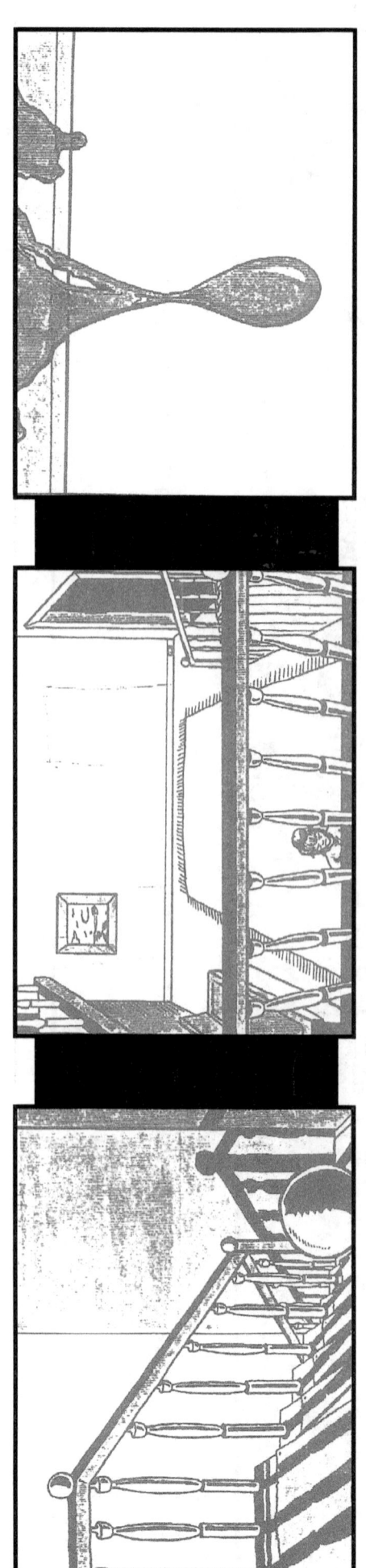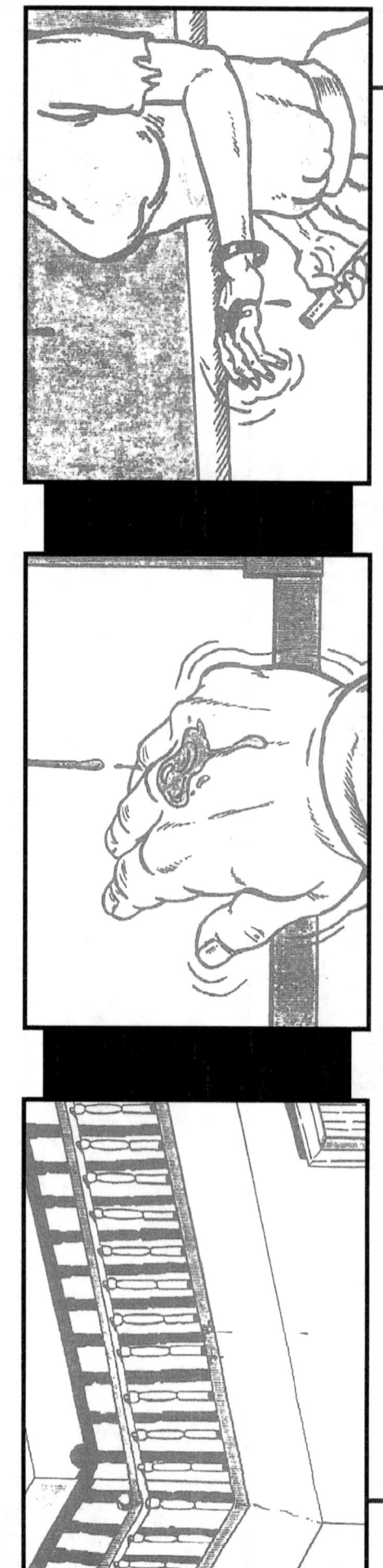

Barbara hears a noise upstairs and wanders into the hallway looking up at the balcony. Suddenly a drop of blood hits her hand and she looks up to see a dripping.

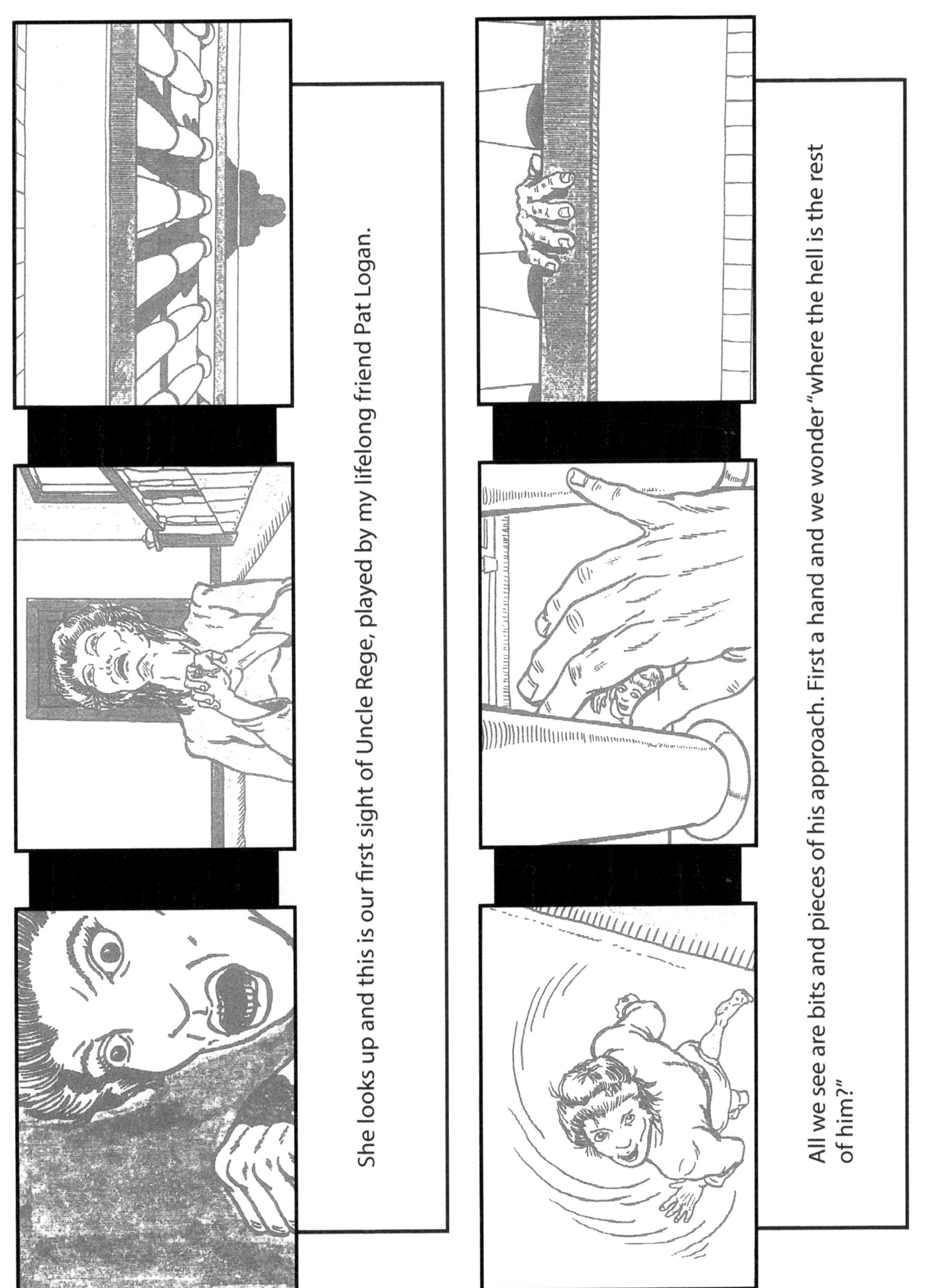

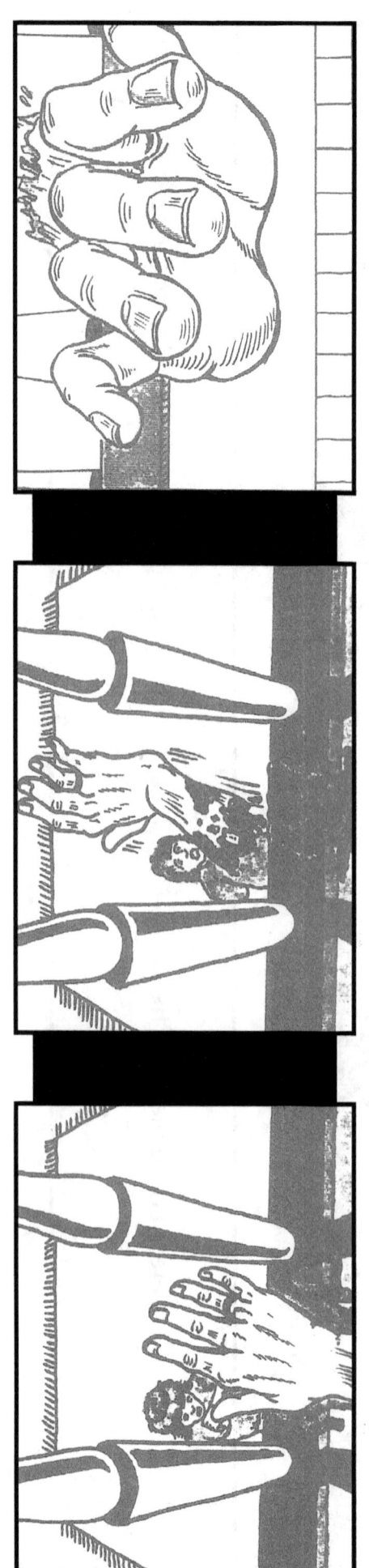

I wanted you to think this is a person crawling toward the balcony, but suddenly we see it is a severed hand that Uncle Rege seems to be pushing ahead with his feet as he walks. It falls onto Barbara sending her to the floor.

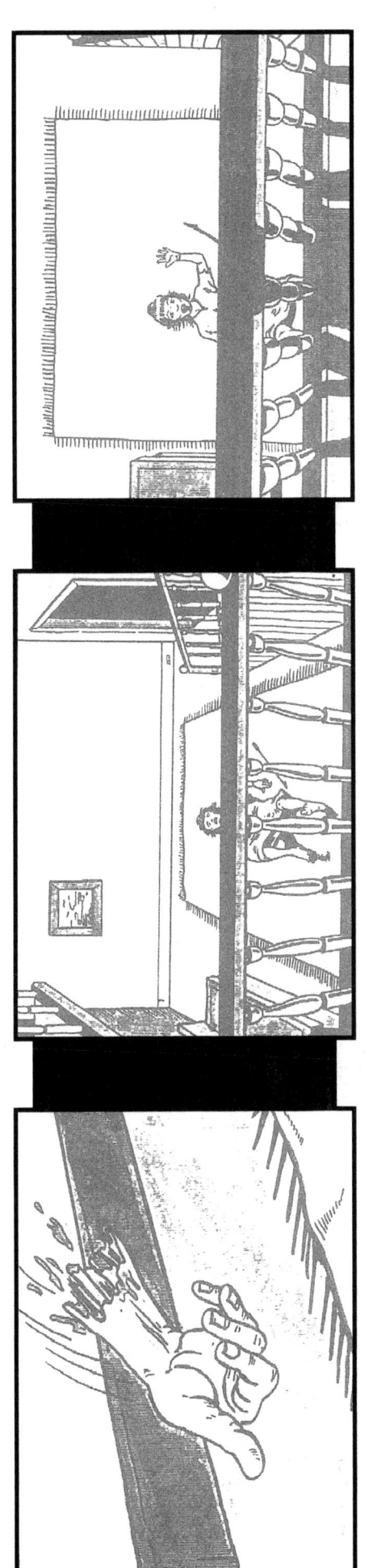

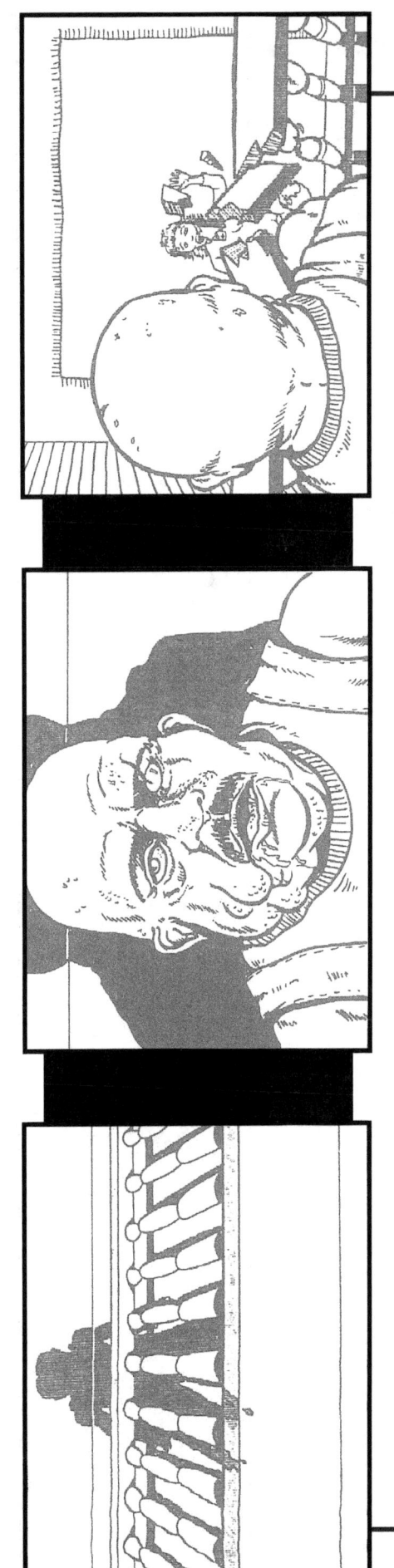

This is the approach of Uncle Rege before he crashes through the railing. Pat Logan did that stunt himself just two weeks after being released from the hospital, after his motorcycle accident that cost him his spleen, some ribs, and a collar bone.

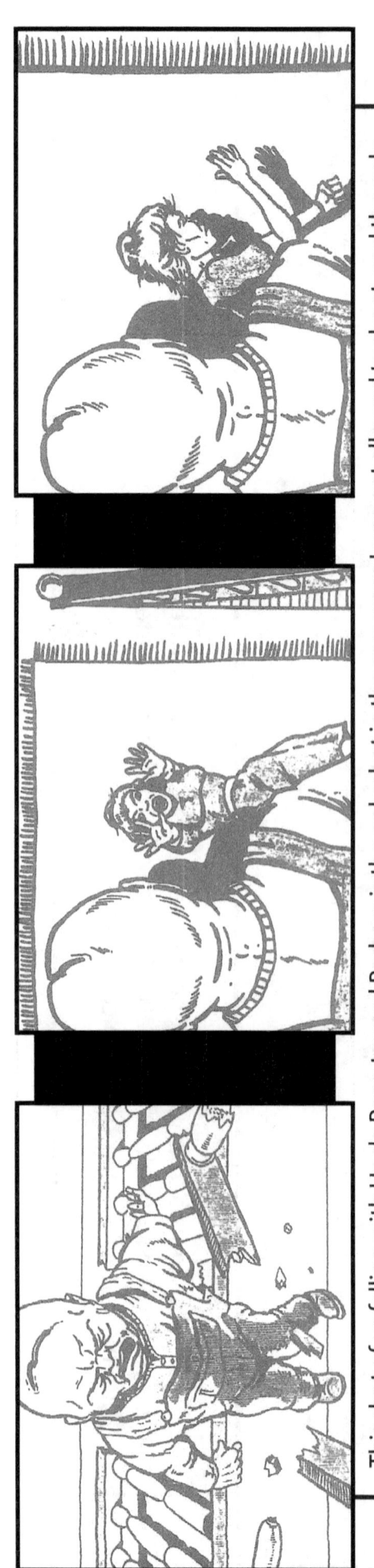

This shot of us falling with Uncle Rege toward Barbara is the only shot in the sequence I was allowed to shoot, and the only shot in the sequence that Uncle Rege, Pat Logan, wound up not being in. It involved Barbara against a wall that looked like the floor and Uncle Rege would be dollied toward her as if he was falling from above. Some idiot sleazy lying nameless producer told George in Florida that I was planning a shot that would take four hours...so he nixed it. It would have taken ten minutes, but is another example of George being lied to about what was going on.

It was a big rubber dummy of Uncle Rege that falls next to Barbara before cutting to the real Pat Logan in a wider shot.

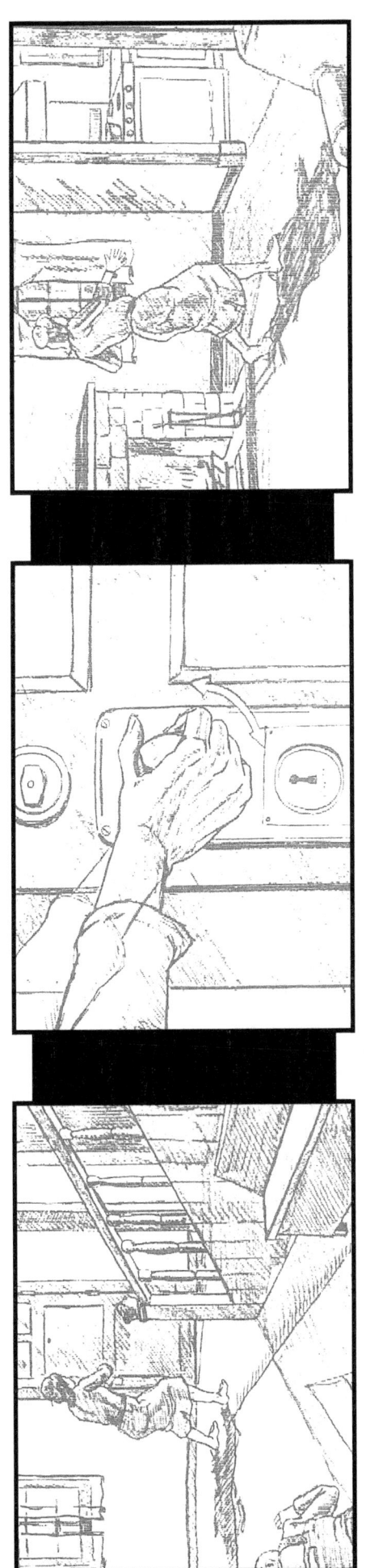

As you can see, when I had these boards made we thought we were going to be shooting in the night. You know....*NIGHT of the Living Dead*. Anyway, Barbara runs out into the night after Uncle Rege almost falls on her.

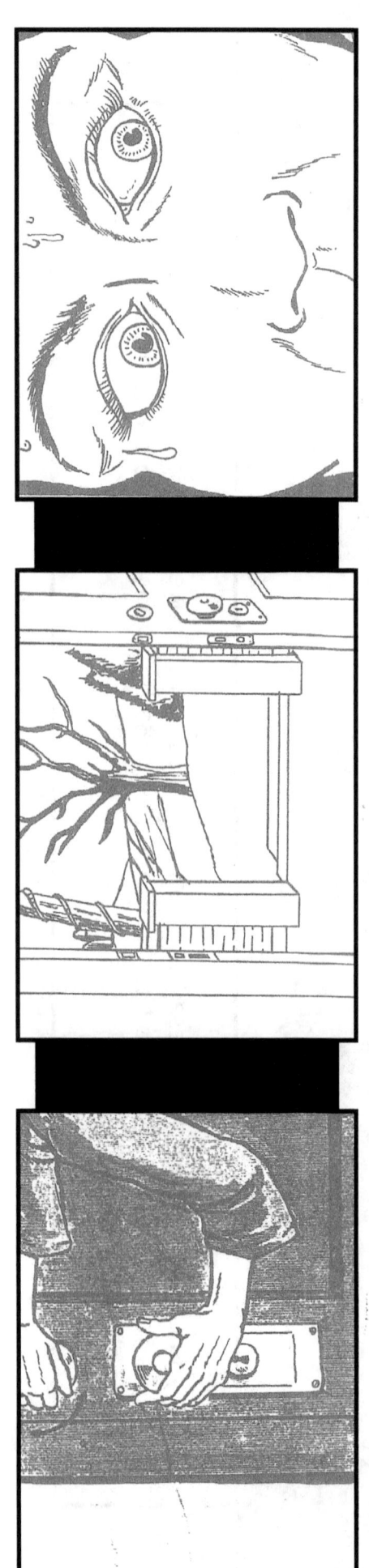

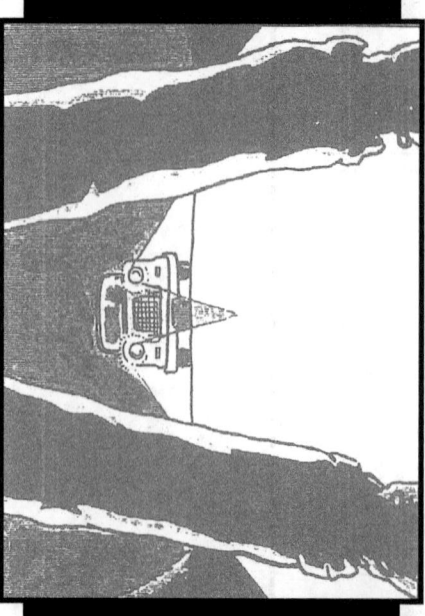
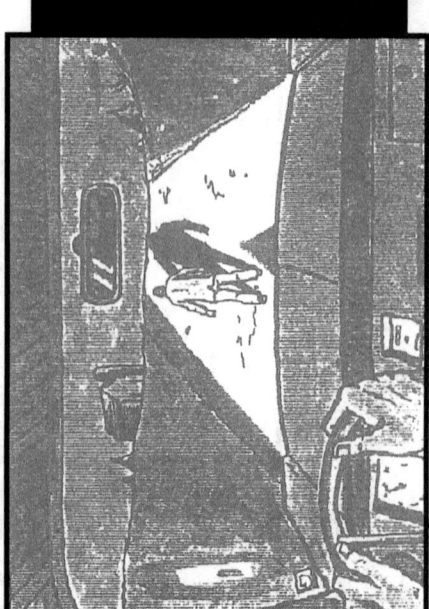

She sees headlights approaching and it turns out to be a truck that smashes into the Dirk Zombie. That's his name. This was a lifesize dummy of Dyrk Ashton, a friend of a friend.

The introduction of Ben. This is what you see in the film. I wanted to introduce him slowly. The first things you see are his feet and the crowbar. I wanted to be behind him as he approaches Barbara.

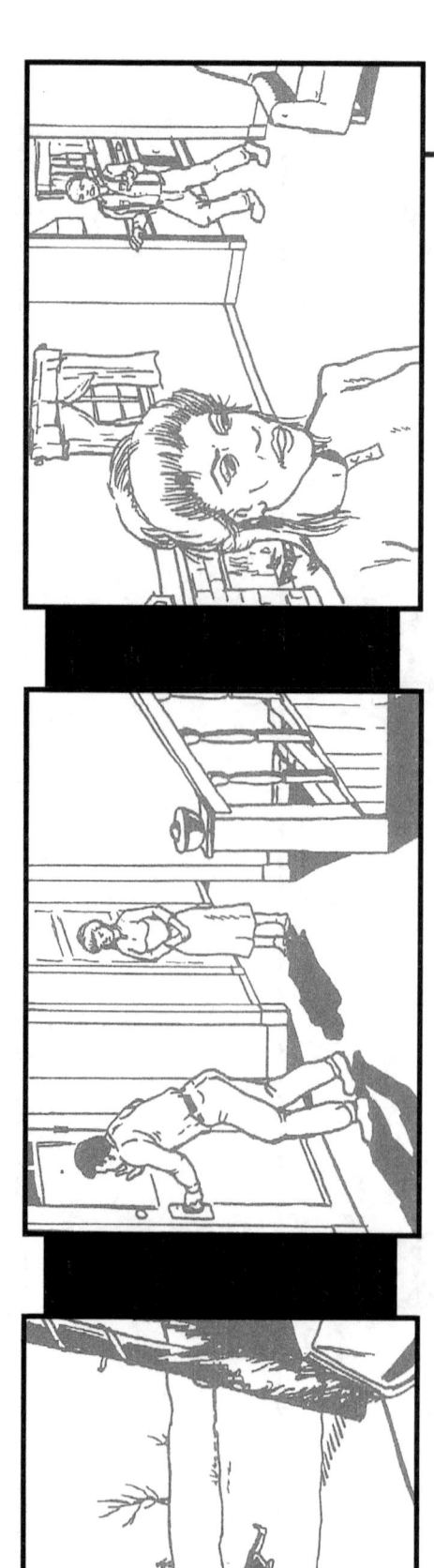
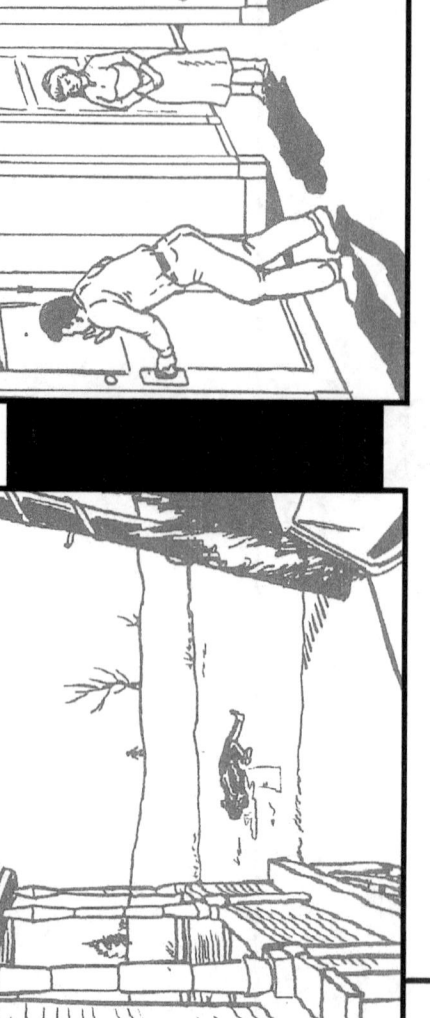

It's her point of view that reveals him and at the same time a zombie is approaching from the kitchen. We called him the Farmer Zombie, played by John Hamilton.

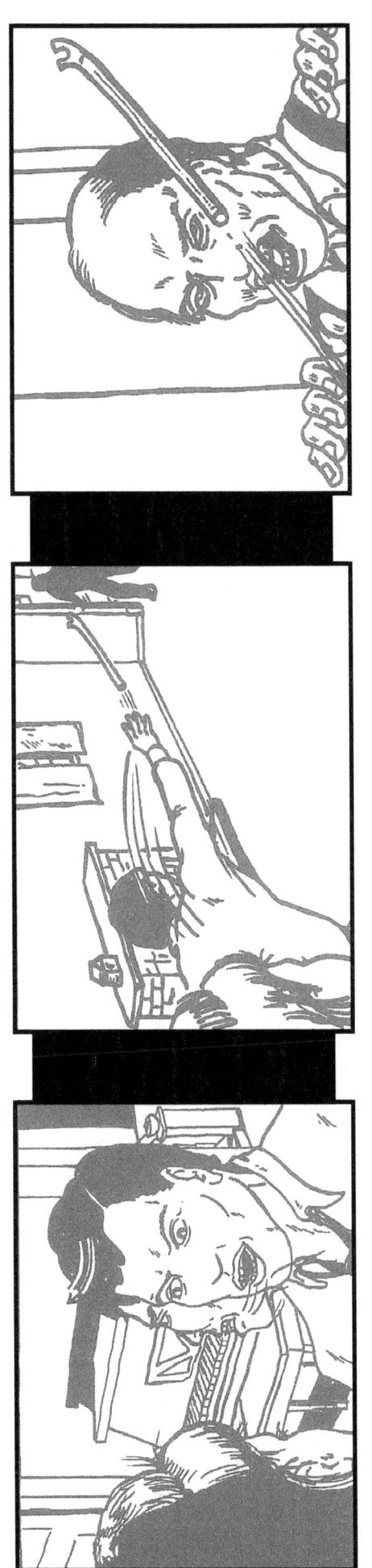
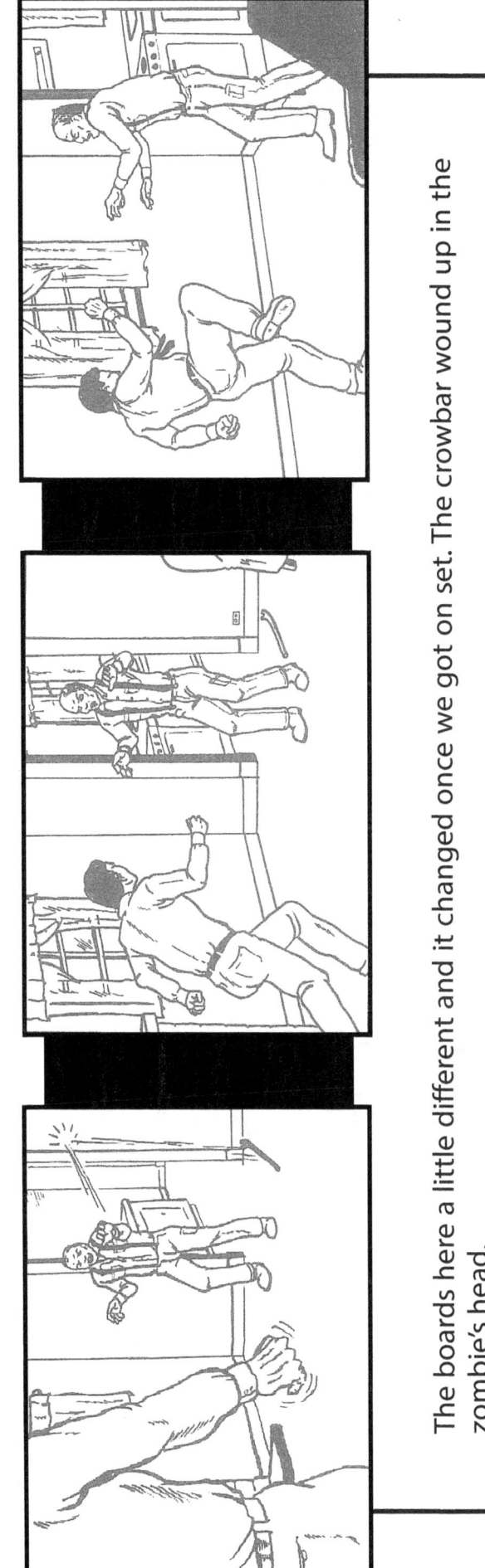

The boards here a little different and it changed once we got on set. The crowbar wound up in the zombie's head.

When I first thought of this scene I thought Ben would deliver a flying kick to the farmer, and then crosscut to what Barbara was going through.

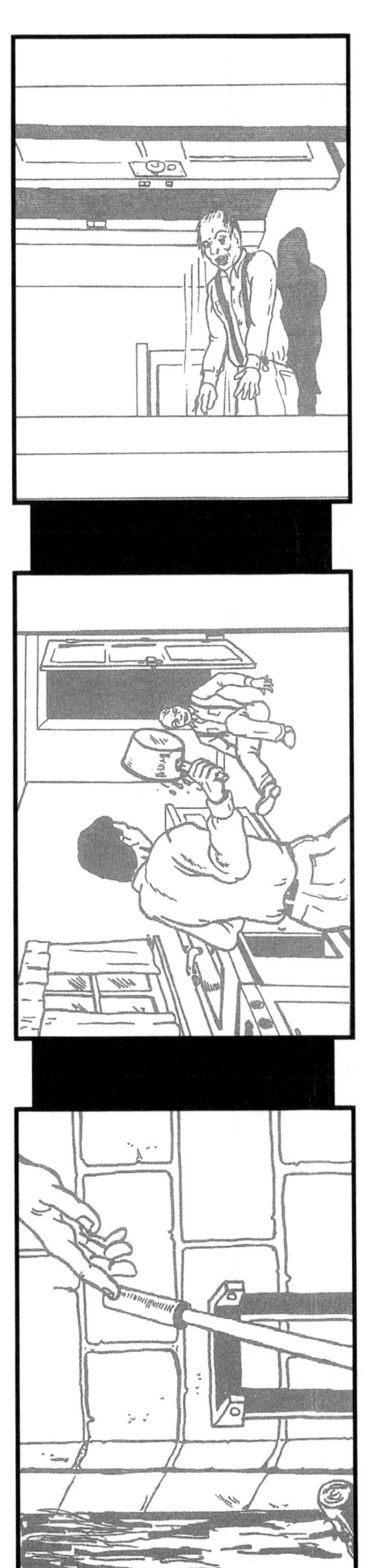
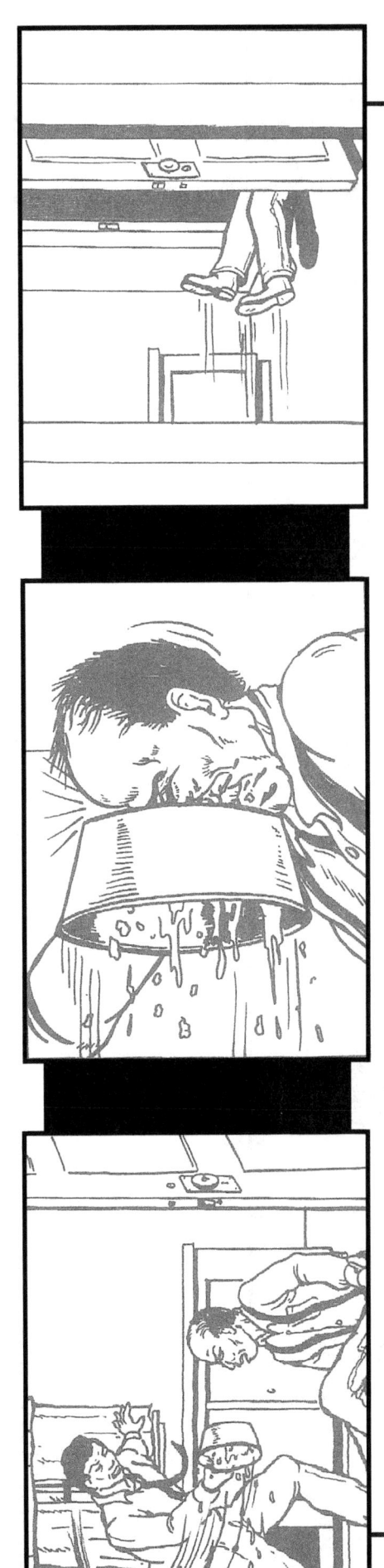

My guys made me a big rubber frying pan because I wanted to see contact when it hit the farmer.

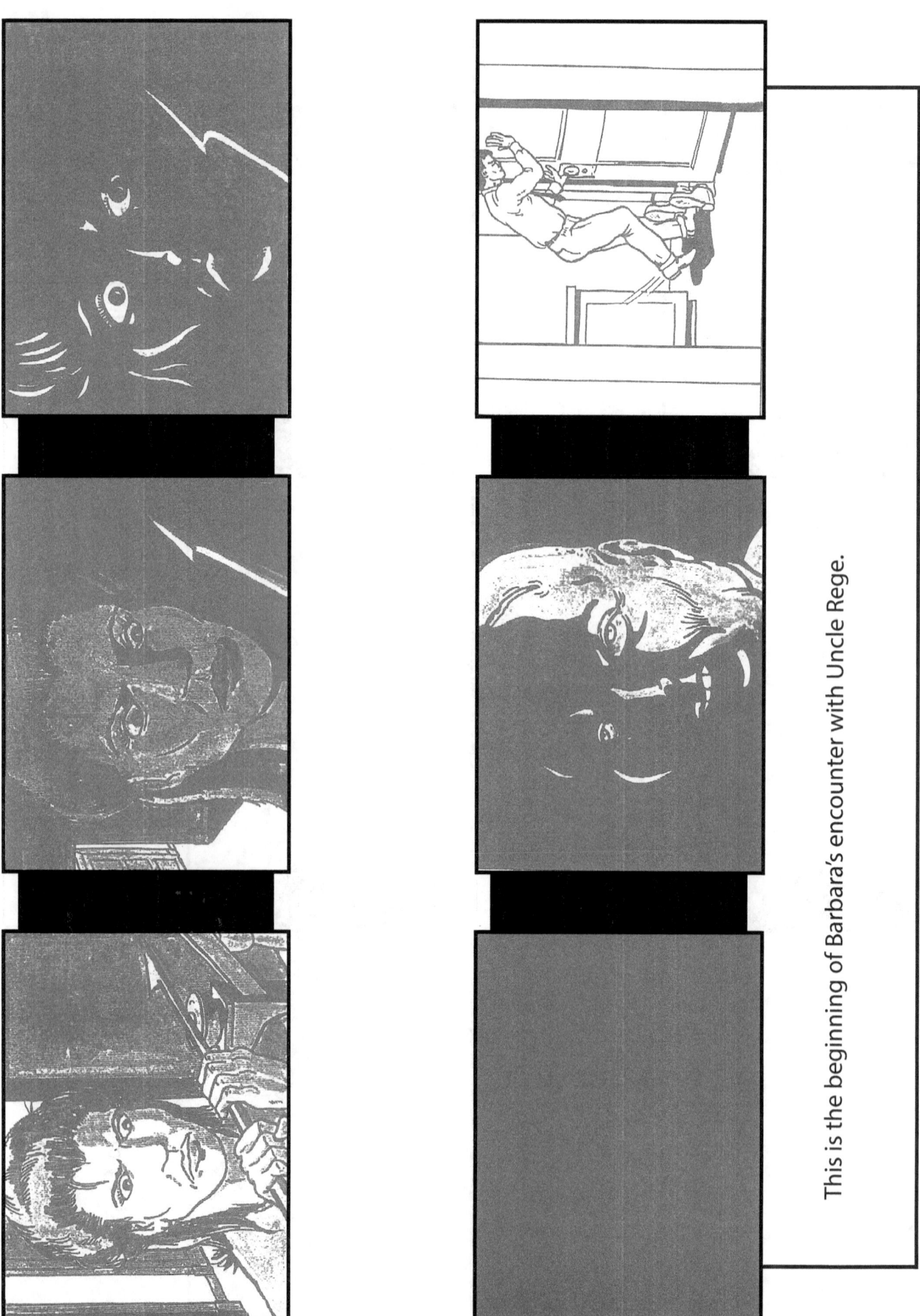

This is the beginning of Barbara's encounter with Uncle Rege.

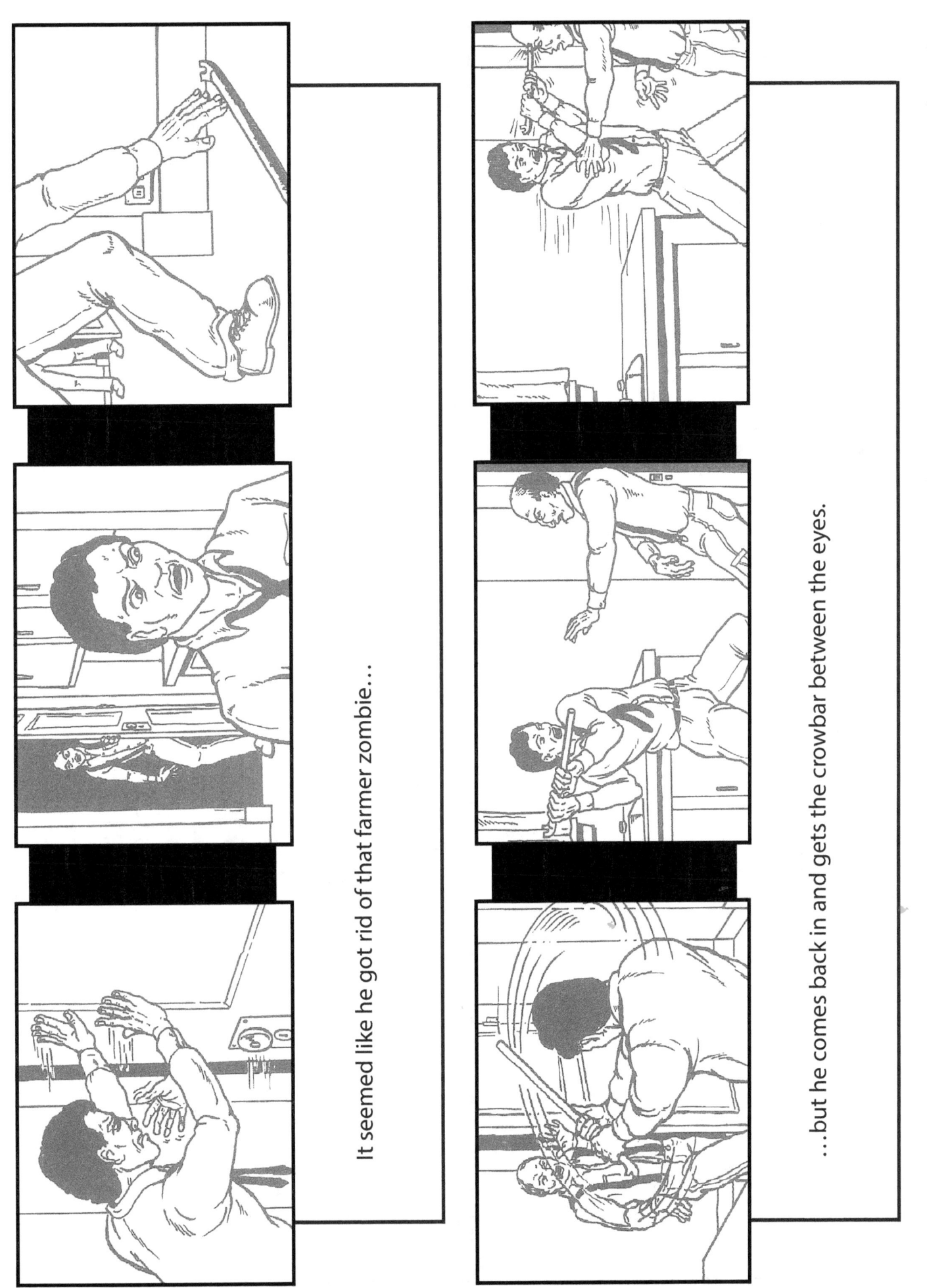

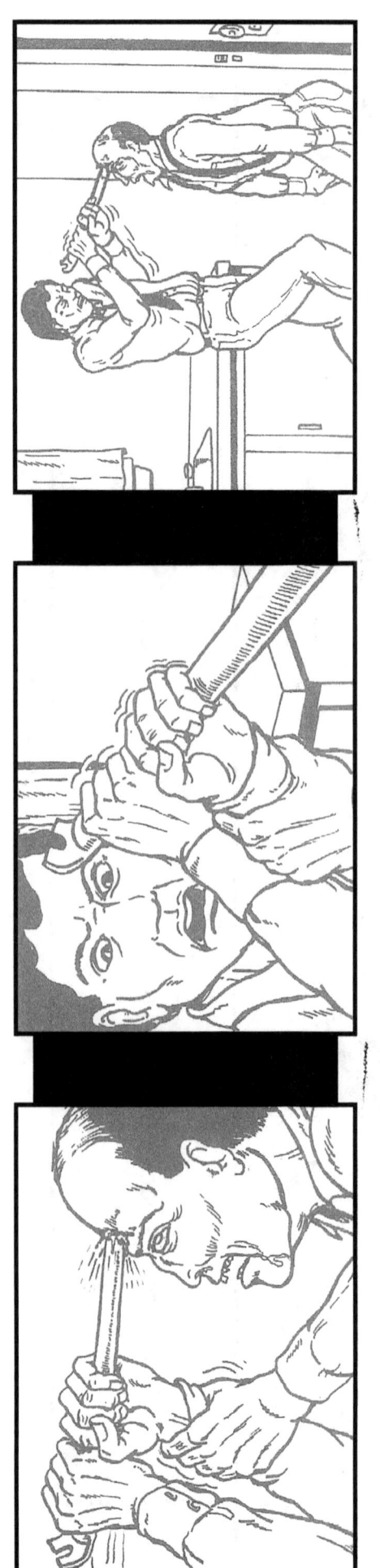

Barbara gets the best of Uncle Rege—and the boards don't reveal the suspense that I created on the set with Uncle Rege stalking her and she realizes he is behind her.

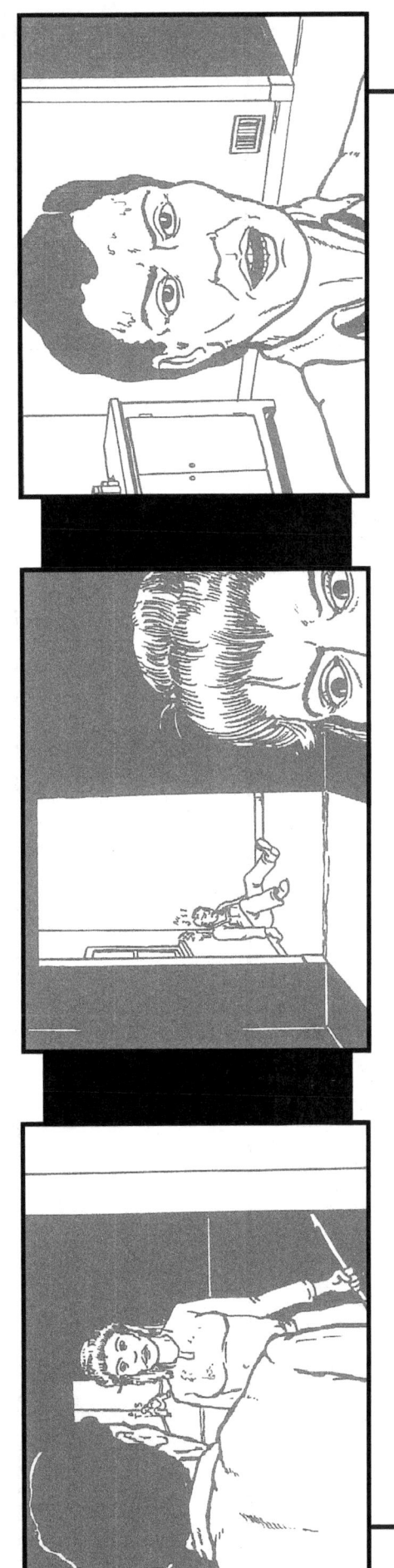

The fight is over, and the exhausted couple relax for just a moment--when they hear something in the other room.

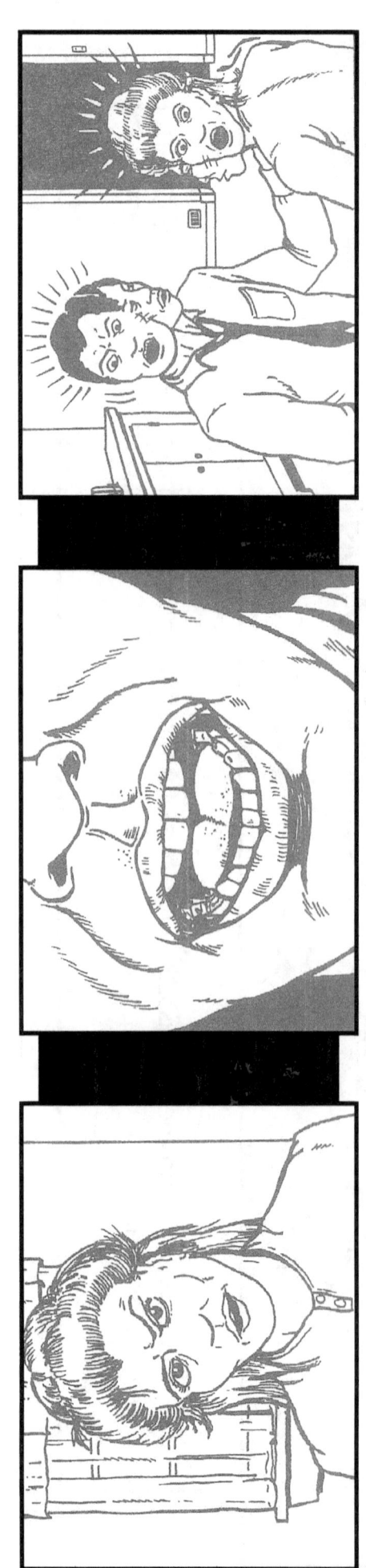

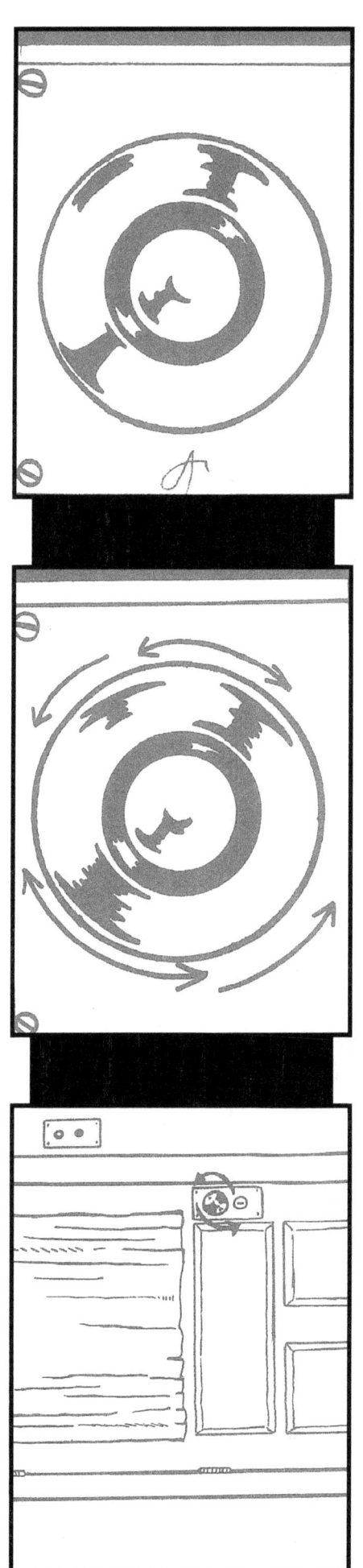
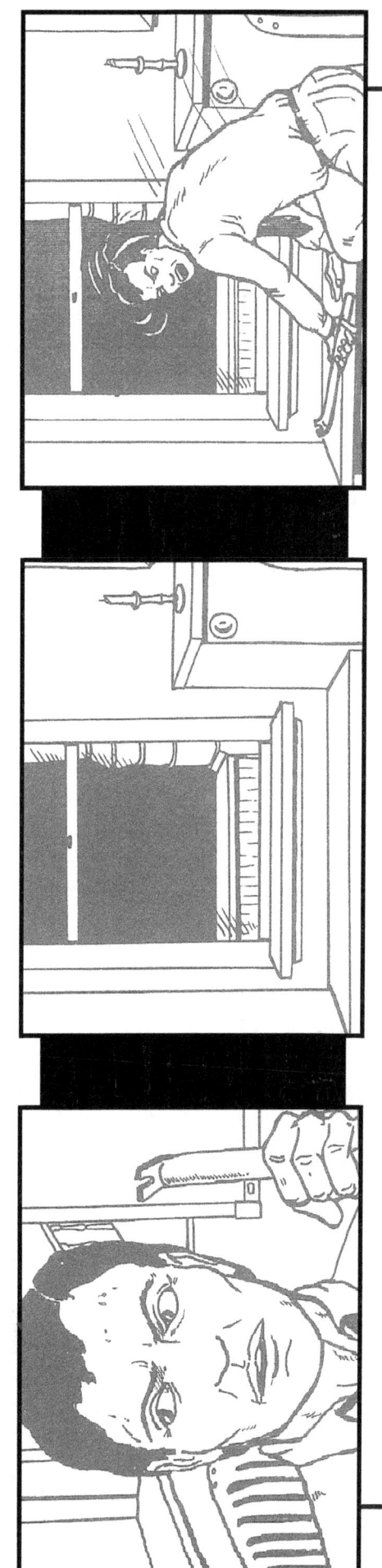

Another example of misdirection by calling your attention to the turning doorknob, as if something is out there, before Ben goes to the window to see what or who.

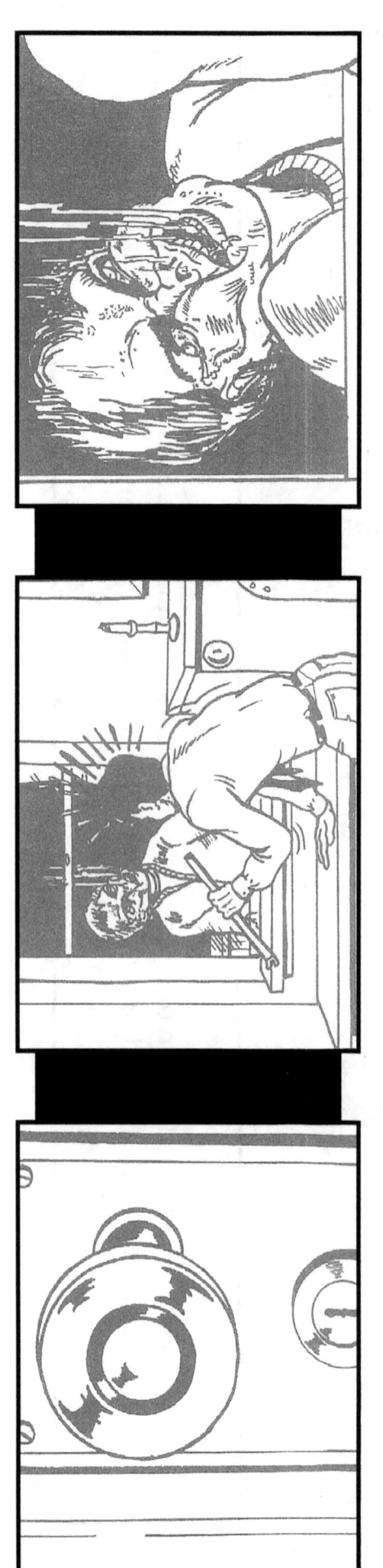

Then WHAM—the zombie hits the window! Chair Jumper, I hoped, and it worked. And this is an example of me wanting to show the impact of that crowbar on the zombie's head.

We put baby powder all over the zombie's head so when that rubber crowbar actually made contact you could see the mist come off him. Scorsese did something similar in *Raging Bull* on De Niro—not powder but glycerine.

Ben goes down to the zombie he hit with his truck, who is now kind of twisted and broken, and wants to put him out of his misery. Dyrk's real body was in a hole and we added the twisted legs.

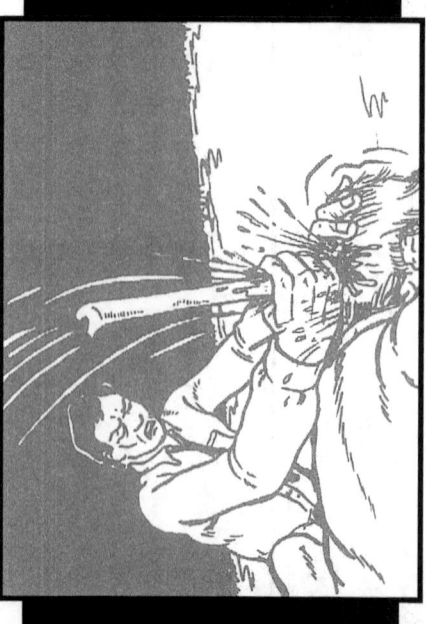

It may sound strange coming from me but I decided to not to show the crowbar crush into the zombie's skull, but have you imagine what that would look like. To complete it in your mind. Sometimes that's better than what the effect might look like.

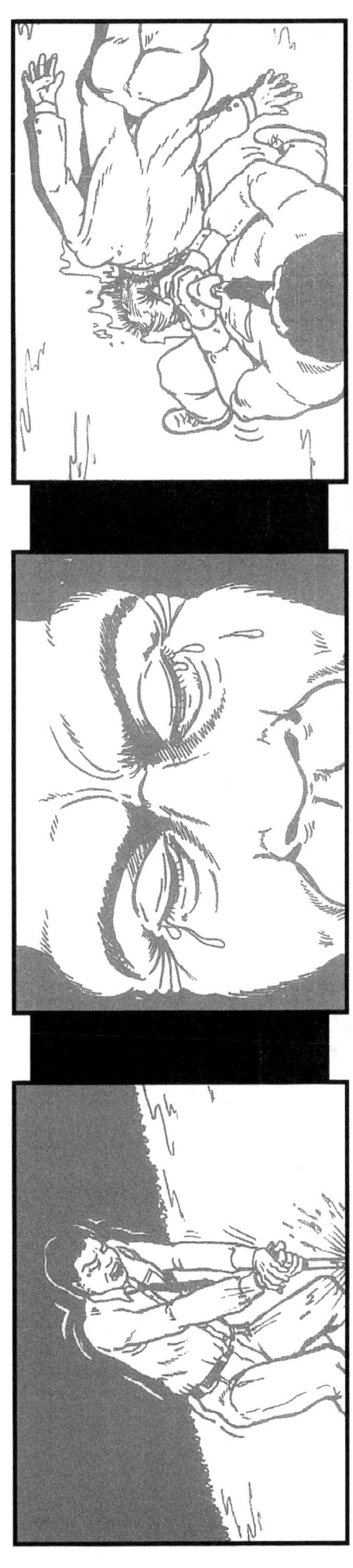

And here's more of *The Version You Have Never Seen*, as I wanted to go from a close-up of the darkness in Ben's mouth to the darkness of the night. No big deal here, but I was told I would need "diopters" and something else—but all I wanted was to zoom into Ben's mouth.

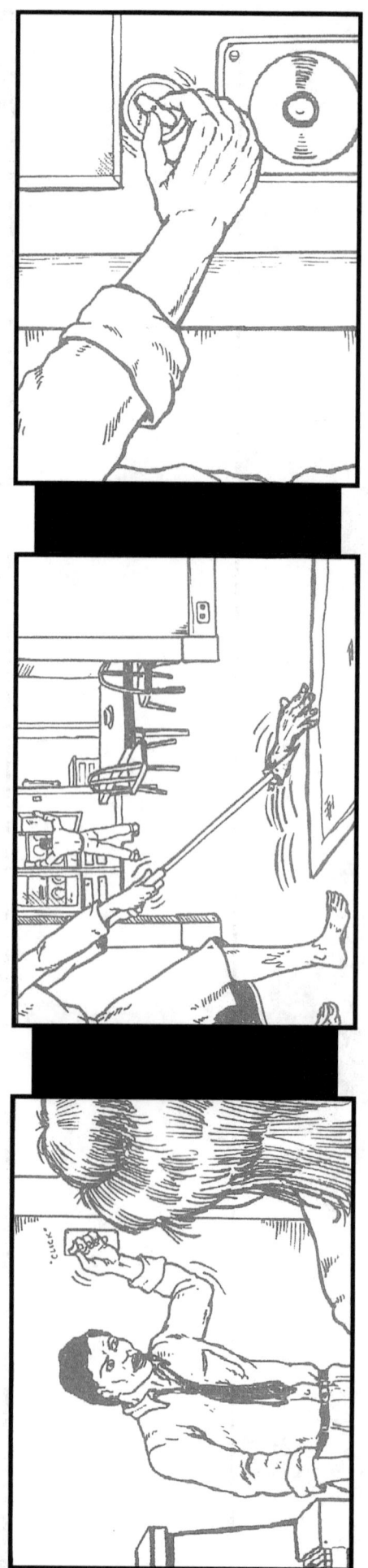

This is all very much like the original with Ben and Barbara cleaning up. Well, Ben cleaning up. In the original Barbara was a brain-dead twit most of the time. I wanted my Barbara to be completely different and have a great character arc later.

Ben is looking around for stuff and hears a noise upstairs.

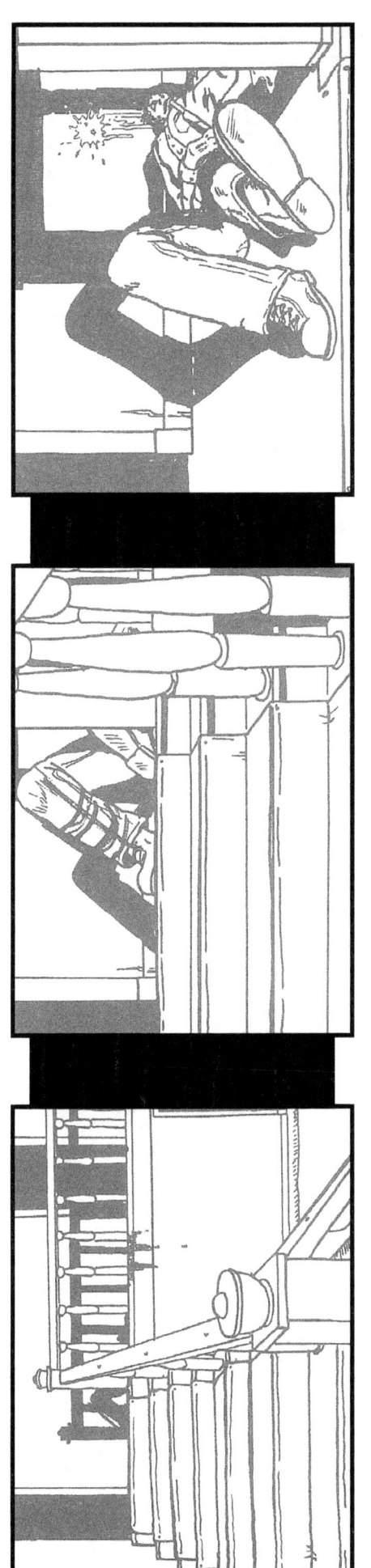
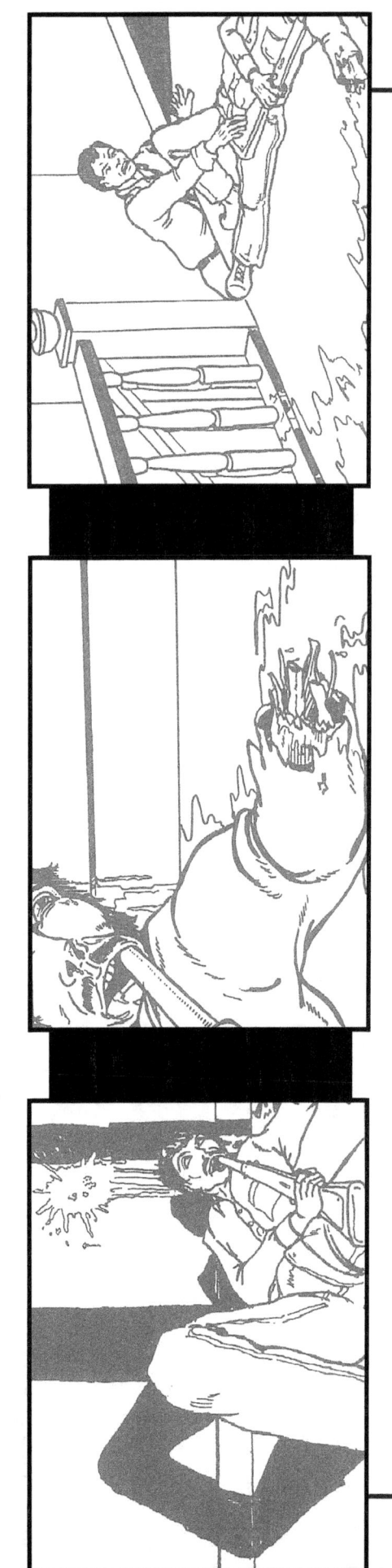

I wanted what he finds up there to be totally different from the original. So it's "Cousin So-and-So" [Cousin Satchel, played by Albert Shellhammer] who killed himself after Uncle Rege ate a bit of him. This guy was an amputee and was hired for this effect.

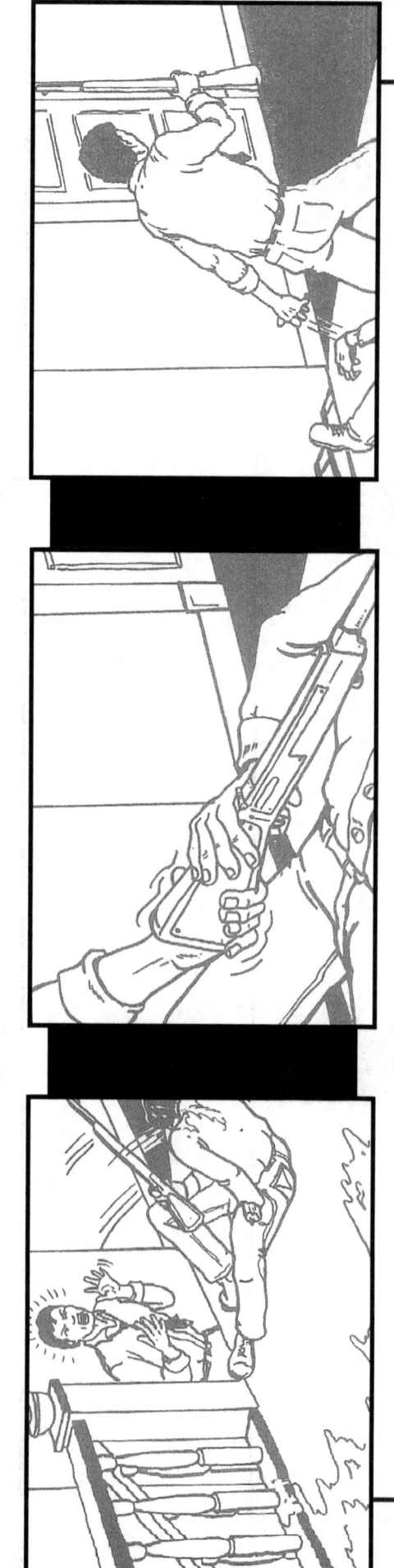

The plan was for Ben to take the rifle away from him and, in the process, the dead zombie holds onto it and comes at the camera. One of those things I was told we didn't have time to shoot and "had to move on."

Meantime, Barbara is minding her own business, and I had the prop people collect a shitload of spiders. I wanted Barbara to look at her hand resting on the mantle and have a spider crawl across it. Kind of a prompt to Harry coming out of the basement door. "No time for that."

This was going to be Ben's point of view, running down the steps to Barbara, ending with him crashing the door into Harry. "No time for that."

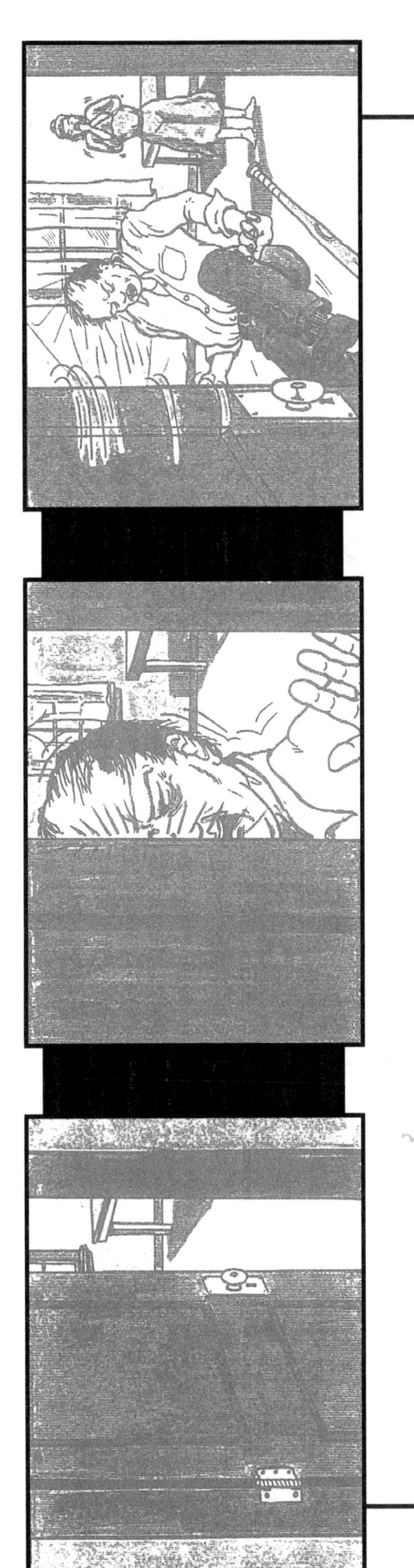

We did do a shot of Ben crashing the door into Harry's arm.

Following the spider on Barbara's hand—we are introduced to Harry.

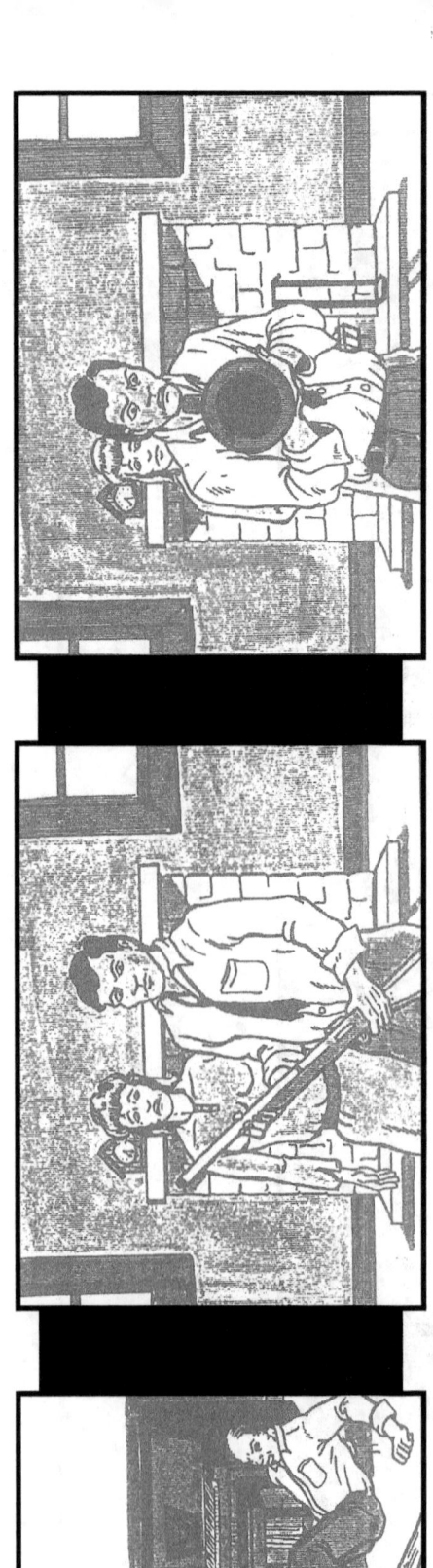

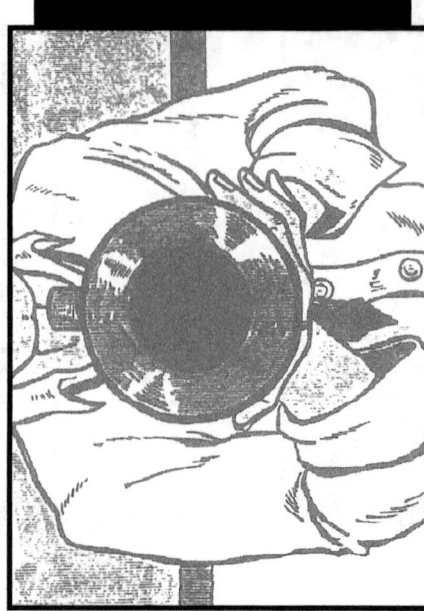

...and the rest of the basement dwellers.

Like the original, Harry and Ben don't hit it off right from the beginning. I even wanted Harry to call Ben "Uncle Ben" at one point. A racial slur. That was shot down.

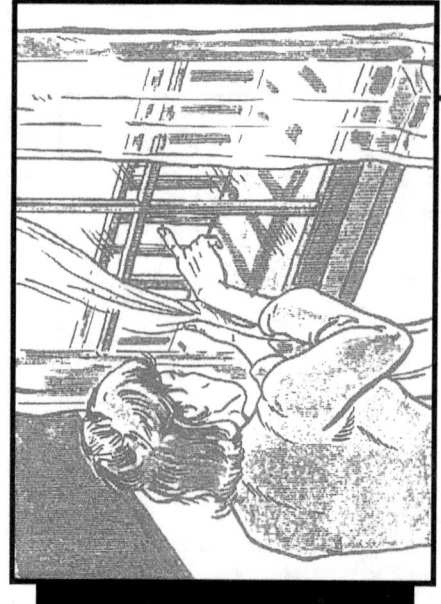

Young Tom tells the story of his cousin and Uncle Rege. Harry keeps moaning about it being "safer in the basement," and he goes down there.

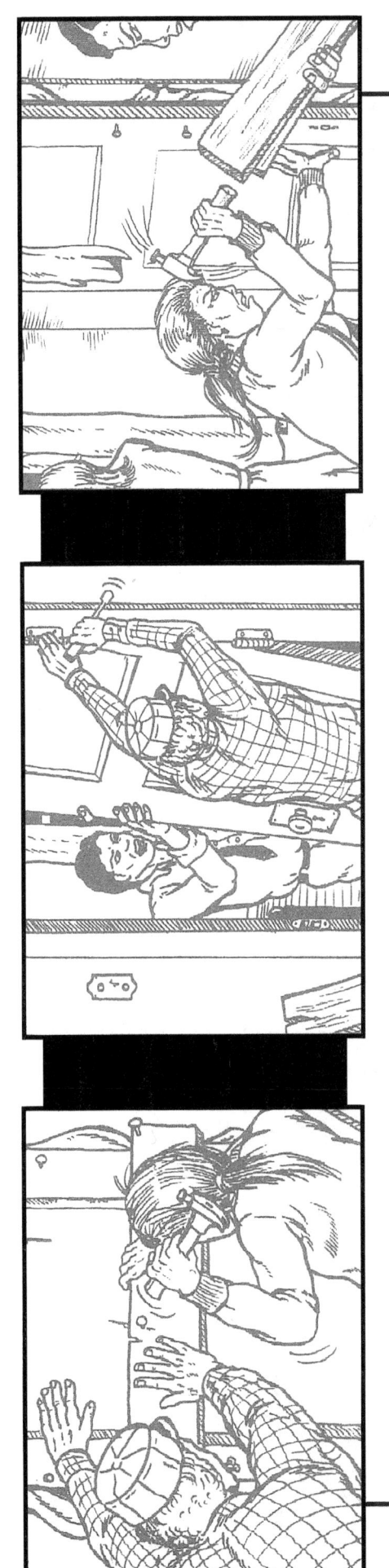

With the zombies approaching the house, Harry intensifies his "safer in the basement" tirade, and Ben and the rest start boarding up the place.

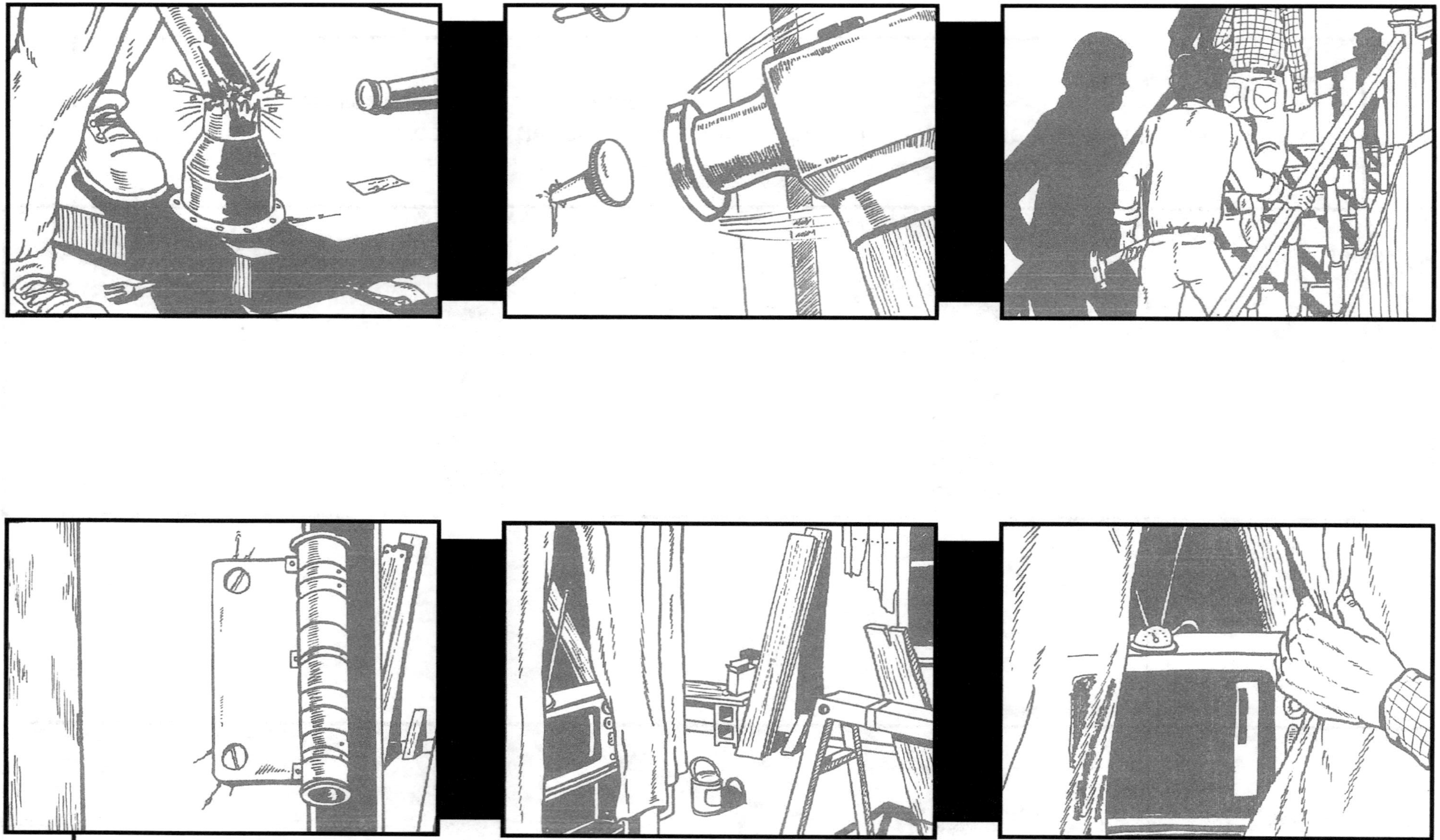

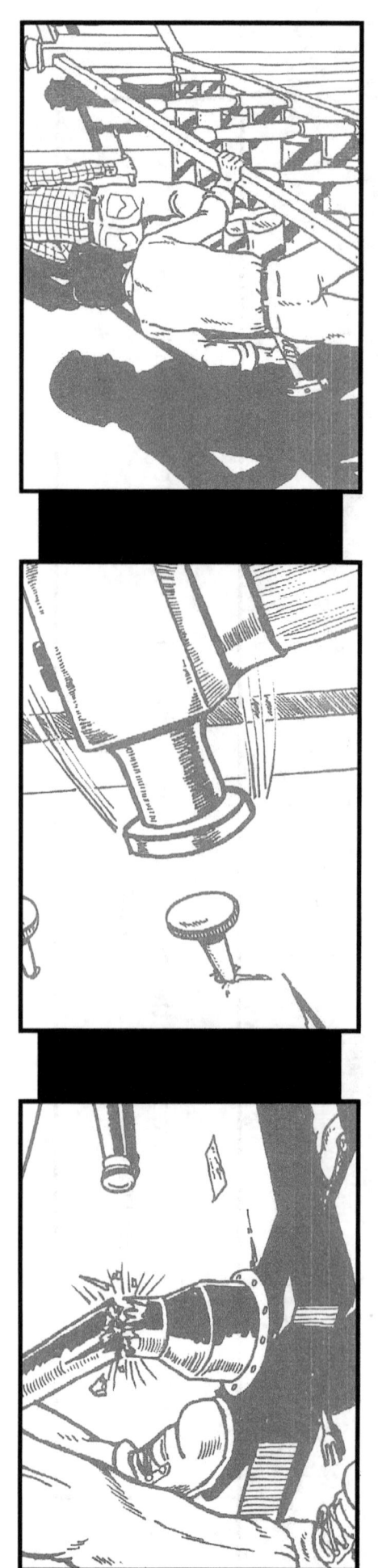

Ben and Tom discover the television.

One of the few things from these boards I got to do as drawn: Ben and Tom tossing wood over the balcony, so when lumber hits the floor I could cut down to Harry, and his wife Helen, and his dying daughter, and show dust falling on them from the ceiling.

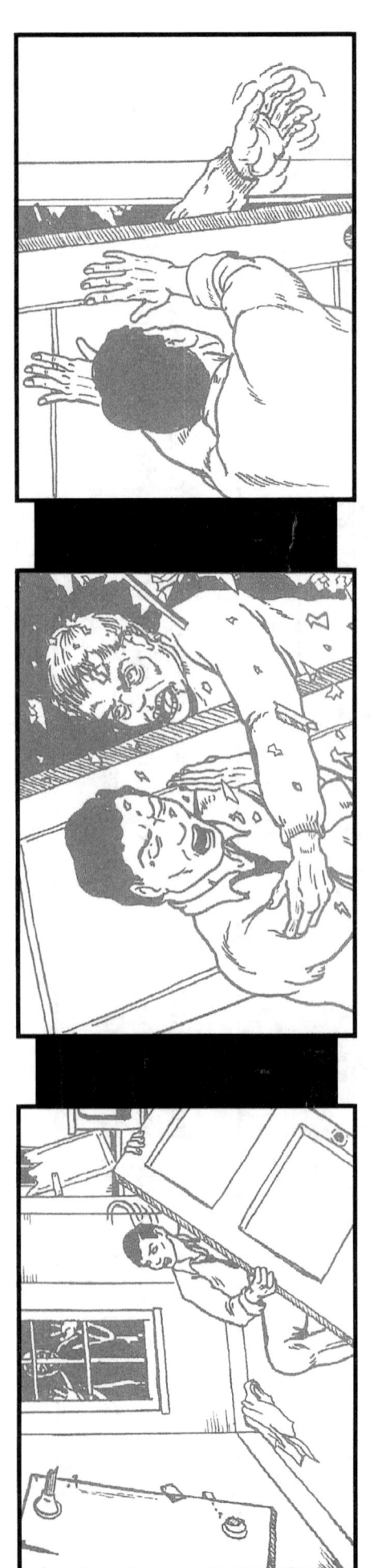
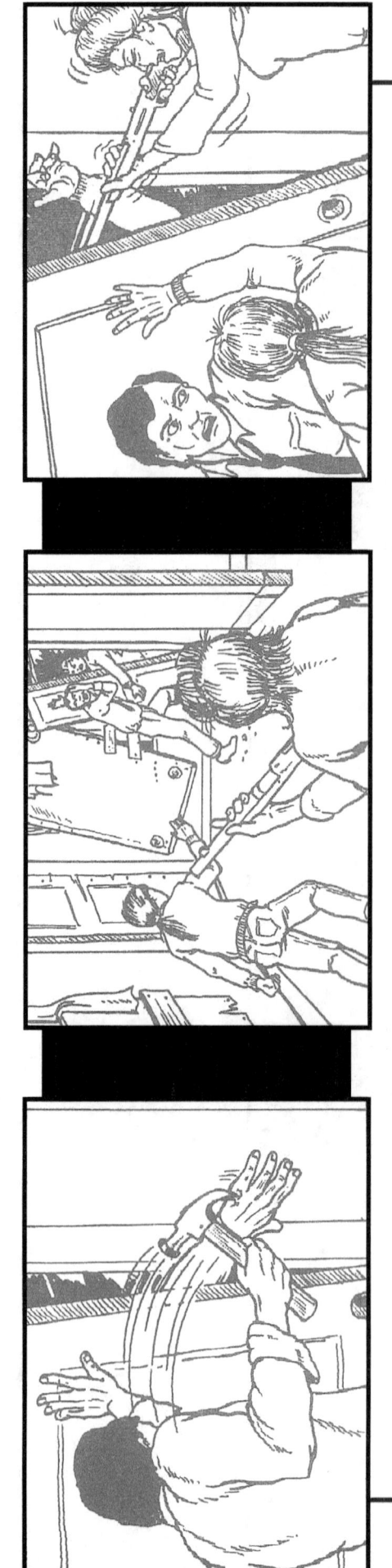

The group is having their troubles fending off the attacking zombies. A standout was Mr. McGruder (played by Walter Berry). This was a guy I was staring at in a diner one night. He was gaunt and I thought he would make a great zombie.

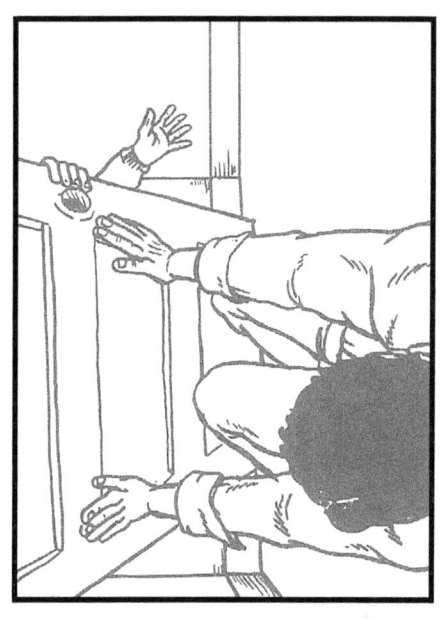

I walked over to him and said we would be making a movie here in his town and would he like to be in it...as a zombie? He went for it.

Mr. McGruder finally breaks in and Barbara shoots him in the back of the head. We shot the hit and the exit wound, but it was cut...censored. Judy makes a big deal out of, "You shot Mr. McGruder! and Barbara tells her to look at his back. She didn't shoot him there. He is obviously one of the living dead.

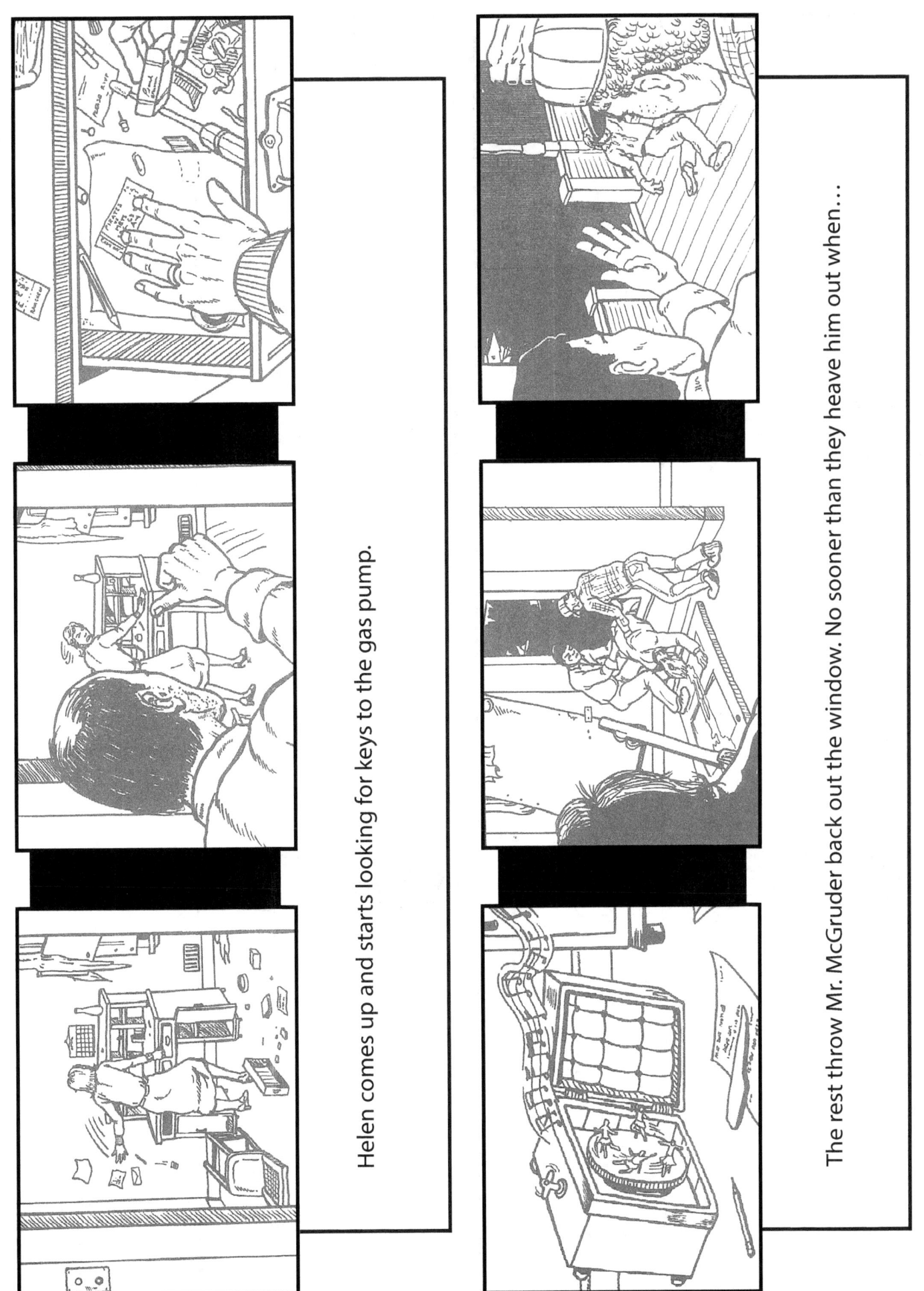

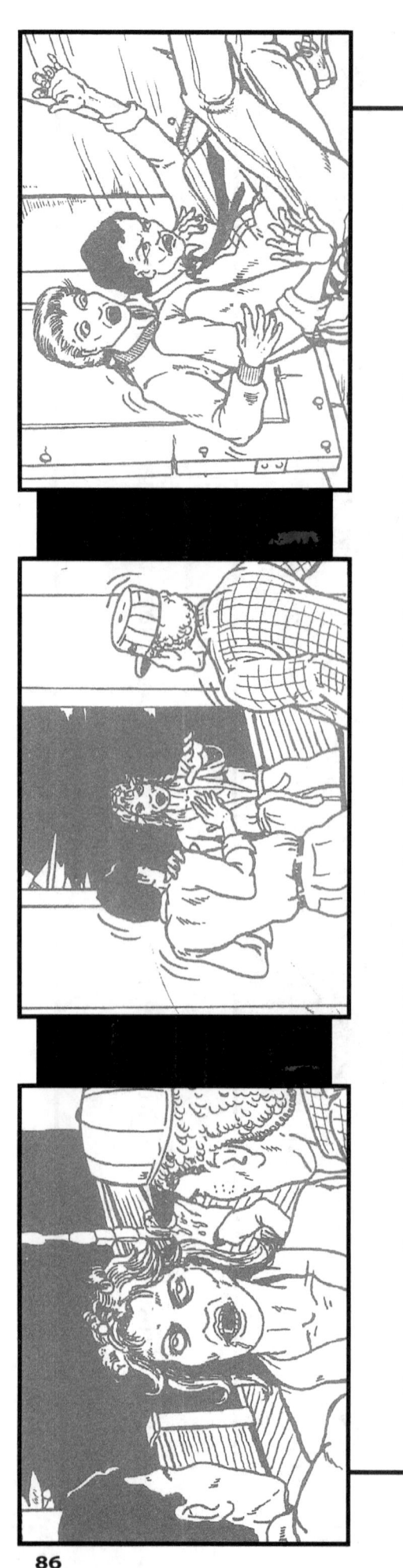

Now we really start getting into *The Version You've Never Seen Before*. A female zombie appears at the window. Barbara sees her and doesn't shoot. She stares...

Barbara comes to her senses and sees that what was her mother in her head is actually the female zombie.

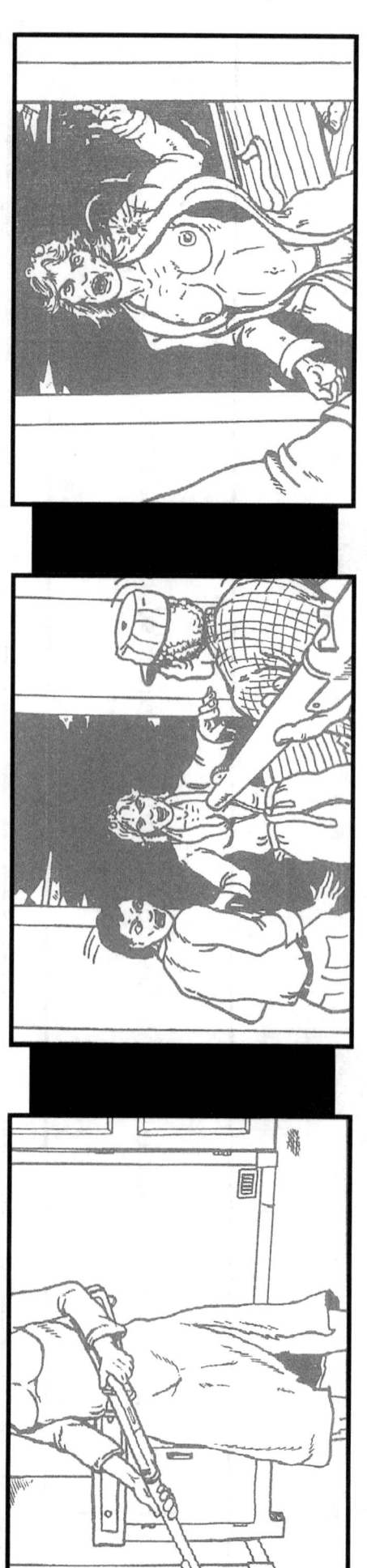

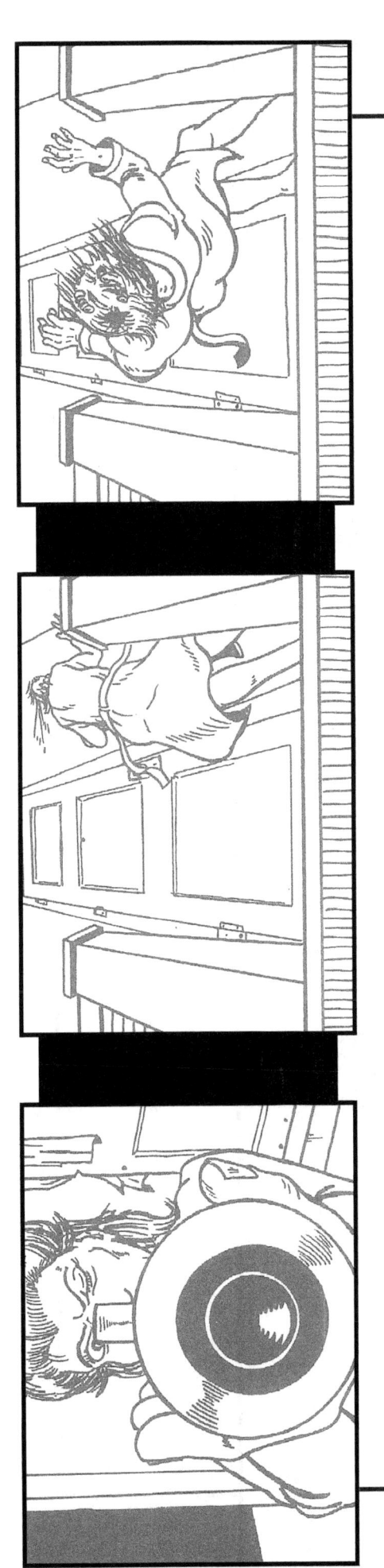

Here is another scene I was able to do right from these boards. Barbara shoots the female zombie. We cut outside to the female zombie's head hit and she falls backwards right into the camera. The only problem was the actor was knocked out.

The squib on her head dislodged from the protective plate, and when it exploded it gave her a concussion. The producers said we couldn't use the footage in case there was any legal action. That's why in the finished movie it was a skinny zombie, played by Charles Crawley, who gets shot in his bare chest a few times. He was a cab driver I invited to the set to be a zombie. His head exit wound was one of many that were censored.

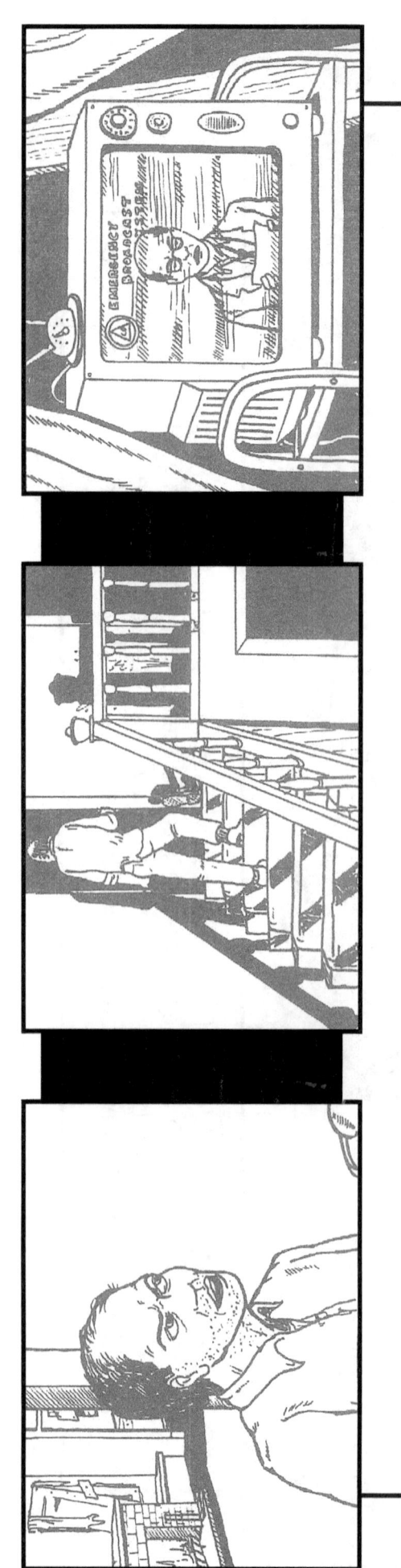

You know the scene. Harry and Ben fight over the television.

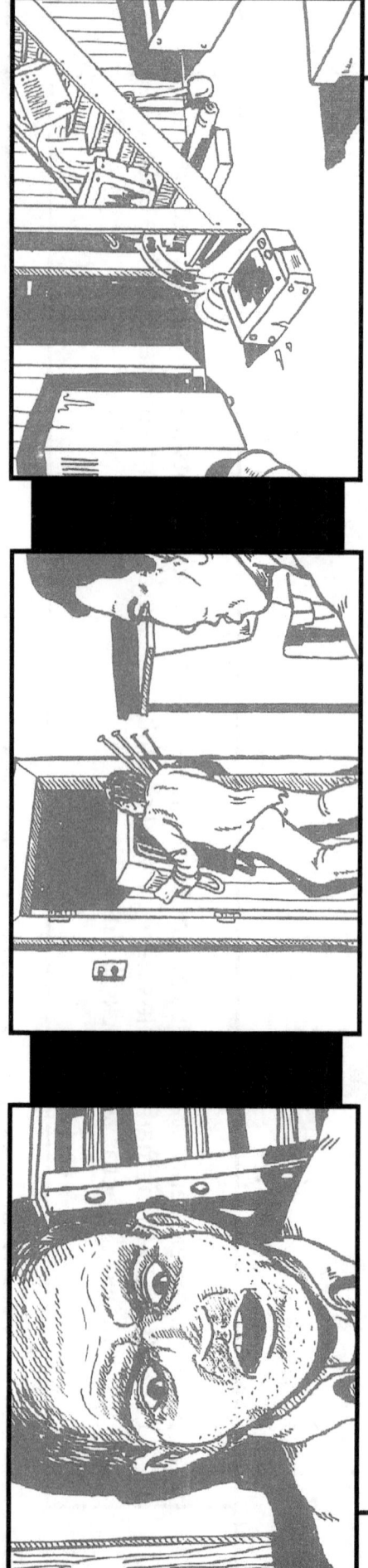

Harry wants it in the basement and it does get down there...shattered.

They all go outside thinking the gas pump keys are in Uncle Rege's pocket.

The original film had a naked woman zombie and we did too in mine, but I also wanted a naked man...and we got it. Barbara shoots him.

Now they are ready to go to the gas pumps and get out of there. On the way out Ben sets a zombie's head on fire.

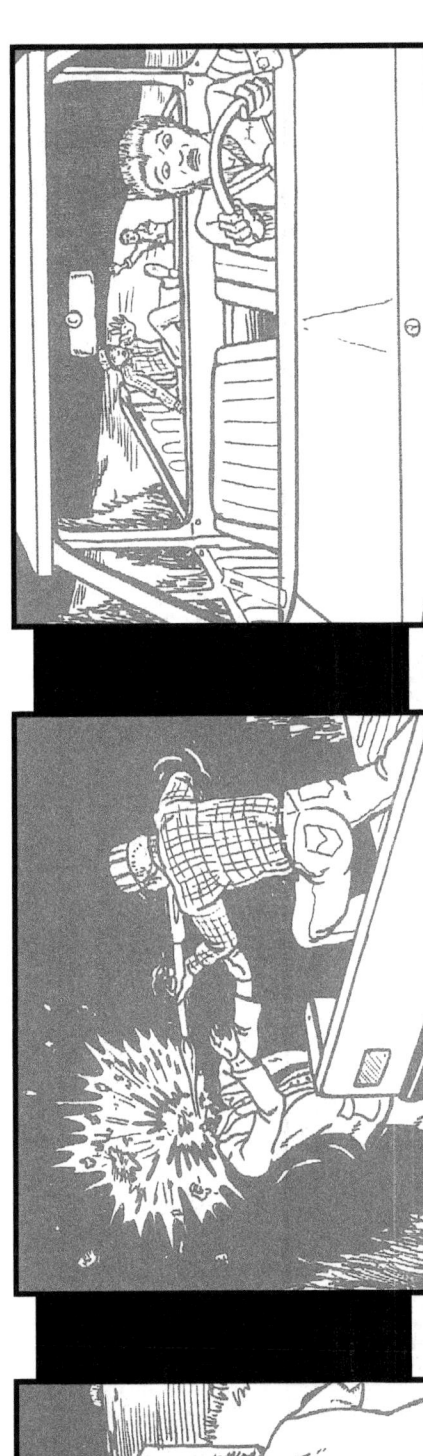

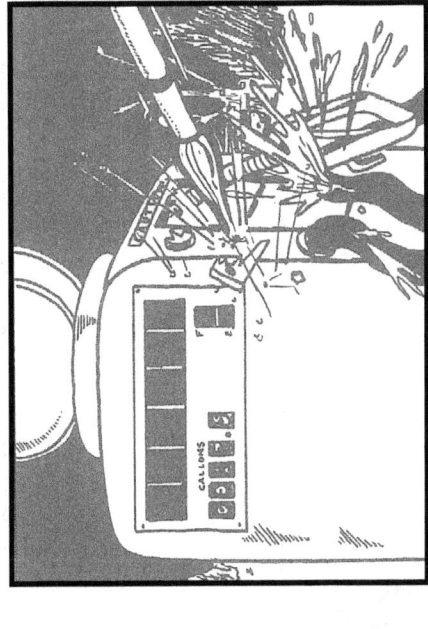
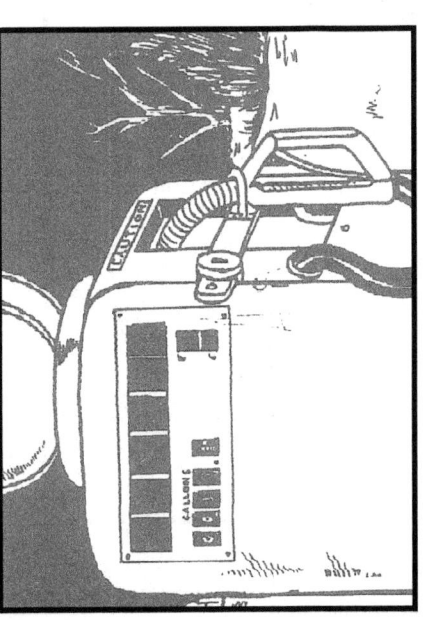

The zombie heads toward the truck and Tom blows its head off. I personally shot that zombies head off. It was attached to a dummy and I used a double-barreled shotgun and fired both barrels. You were robbed of that scene by the censors.

This was something else that was SHOT DOWN before we even started shooting the movie. I wanted Tom to be accidentally set on fire and it is his flaming body that explodes the gas pump. And him. And Judy.

I argued that the stunt team said it was a "piece of cake" and would not take long to set up. George cut it from the plan. A mystery to me. It would have been awesome. *A Version You Have Never Seen.*

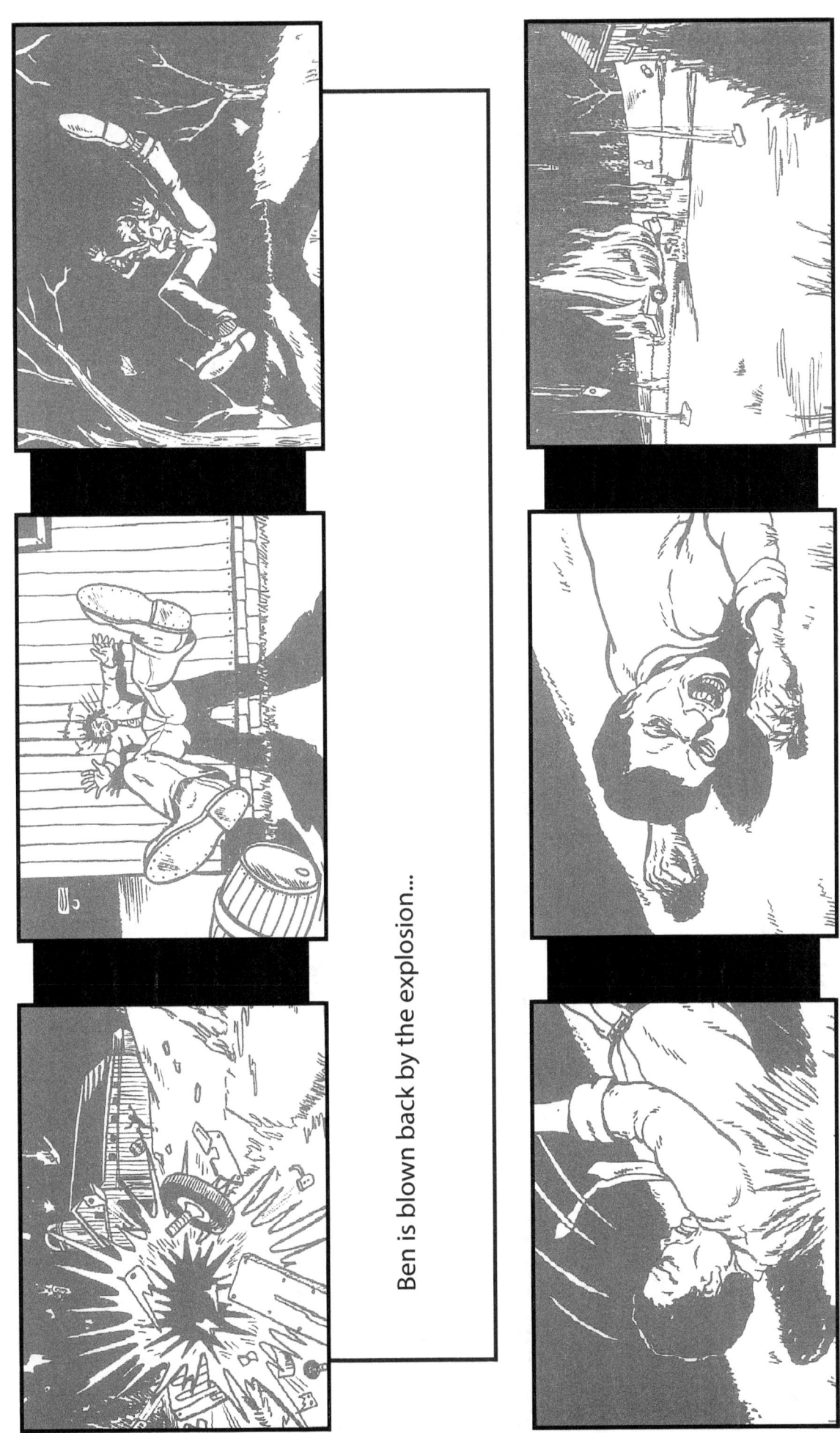

Ben is blown back by the explosion...

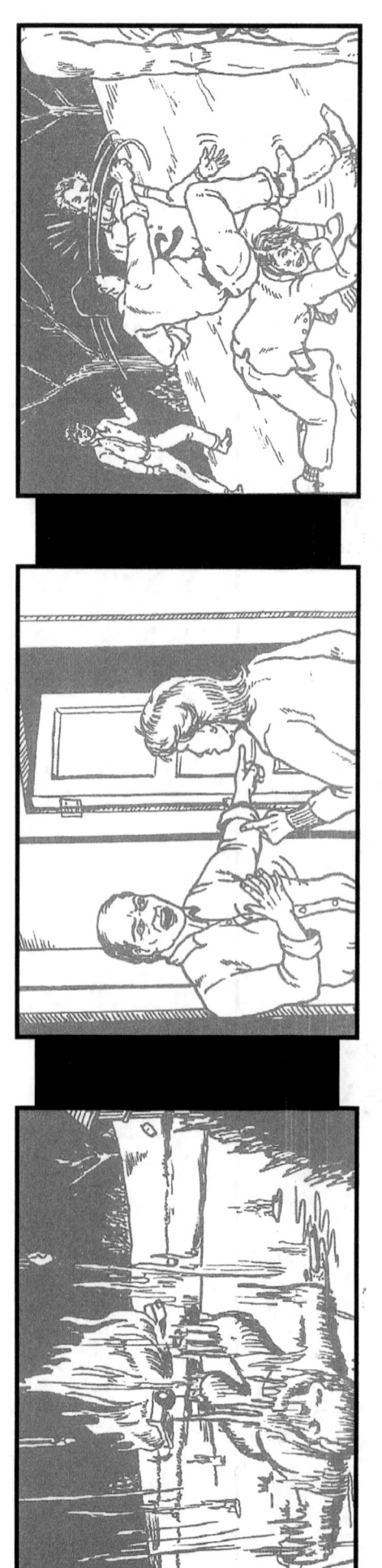

...and fights his way back to the house. Barbara covers him from the window.

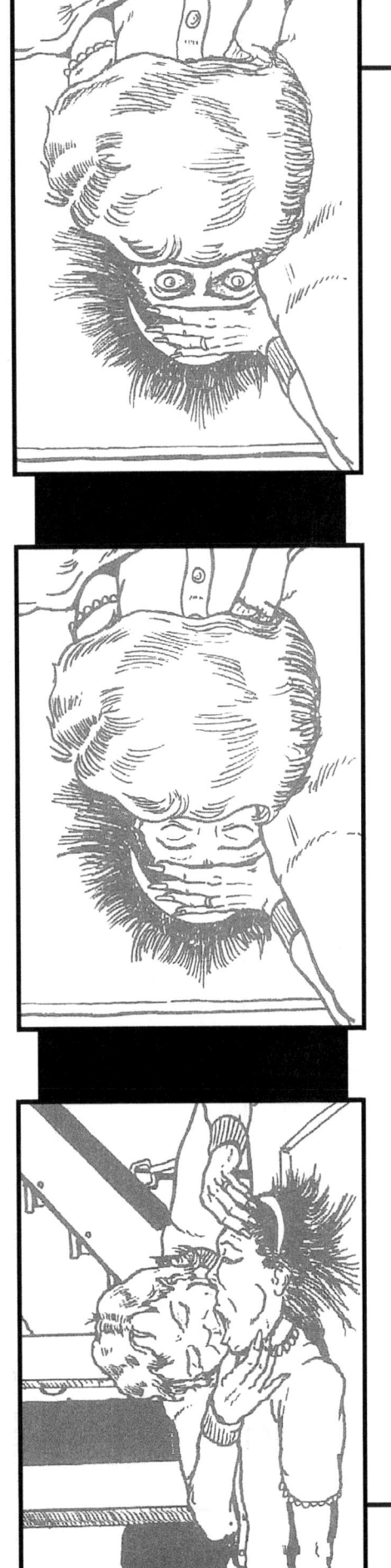

More of *The Version You've Never Seen*. Helen discovers Karen has died and tries to revive her with mouth to mouth. The Karen zombie wakes up.

Karen bites Helen's lip, but Helen gets away.

I wanted to do a thing here where every time we cut to Karen she is closer without actually seeing her move. "There's no time for that."

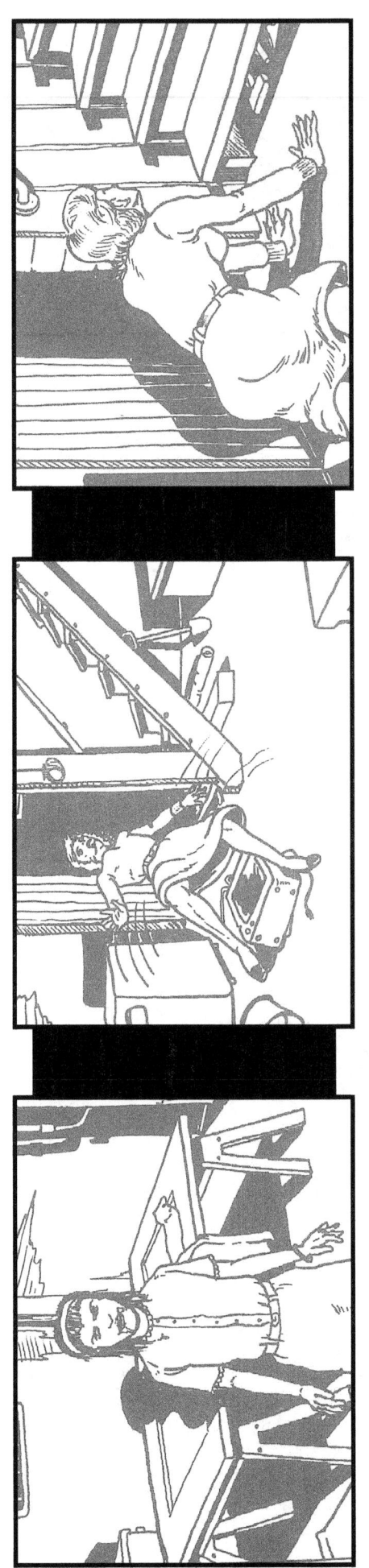

Suddenly she jumps into frame and attacks Helen and bites her as she tries to get away up the stairs.

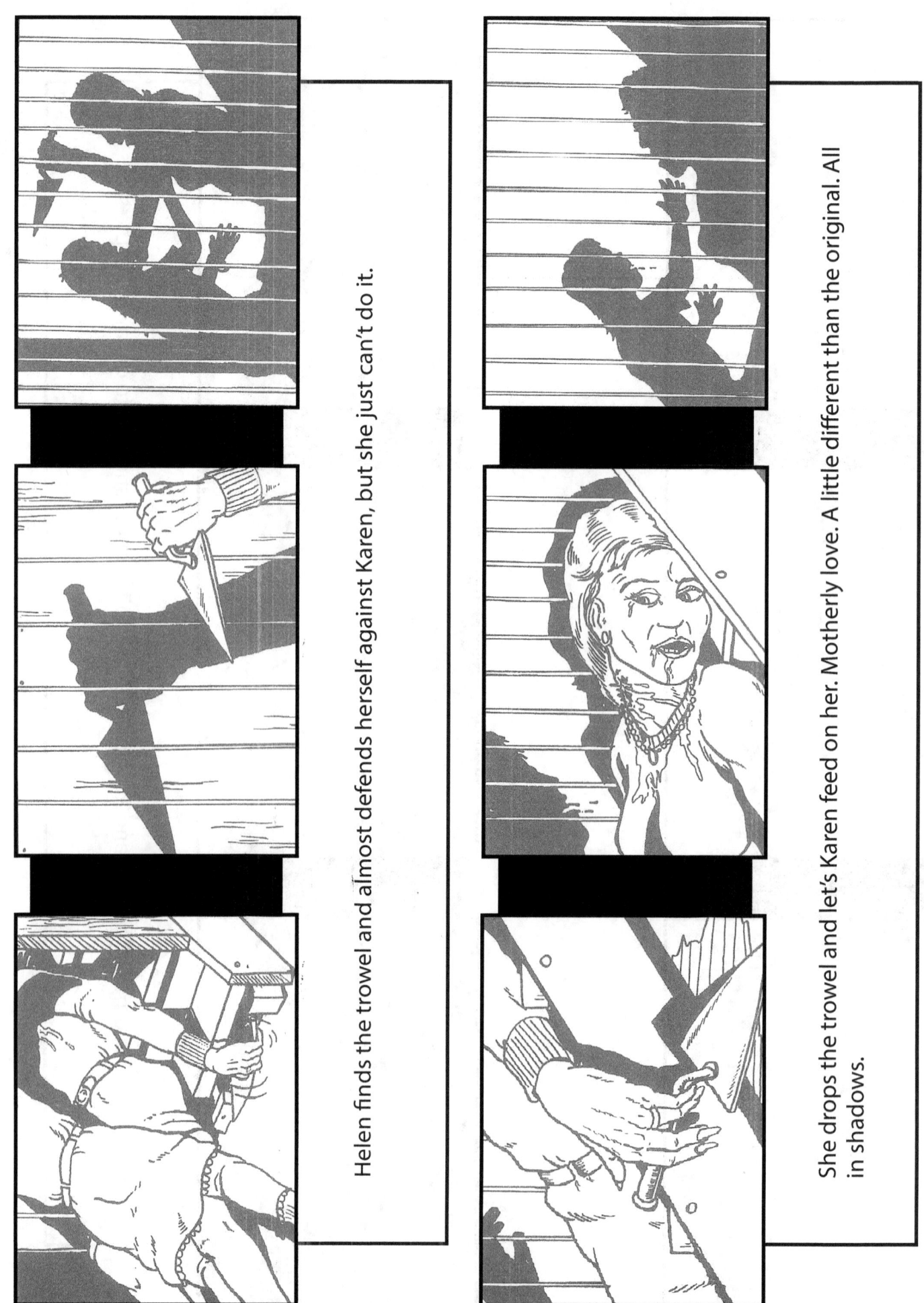

Helen finds the trowel and almost defends herself against Karen, but she just can't do it.

She drops the trowel and let's Karen feed on her. Motherly love. A little different than the original. All in shadows.

Ben and Barbara continue fighting off zombies...

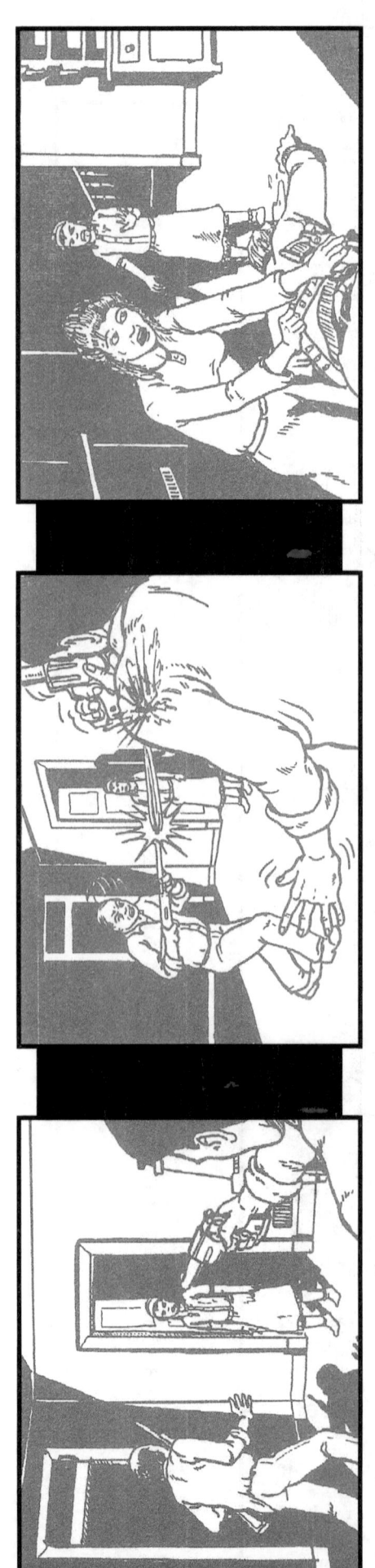

...and like the original, Harry and Ben square off and shoot each other.

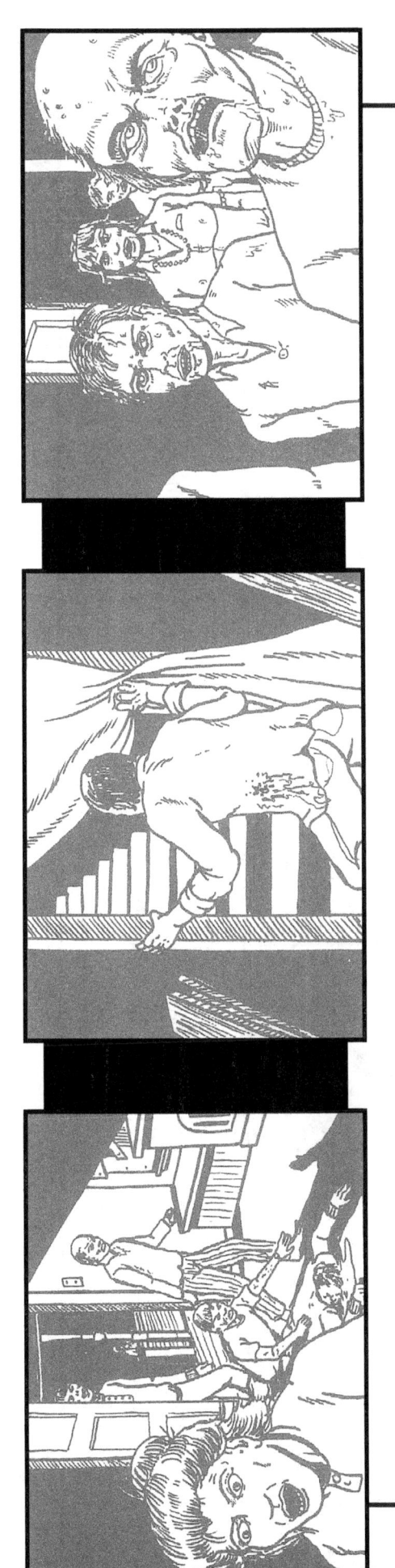

Here's something I really wanted to do: create some suspense here, with the zombies breaking in, and Barbara is in the kitchen trying to get out, not aware a zombie is approaching.

Ben can only get one cartridge into his revolver before a zombie attacks him and the barrel is spun.

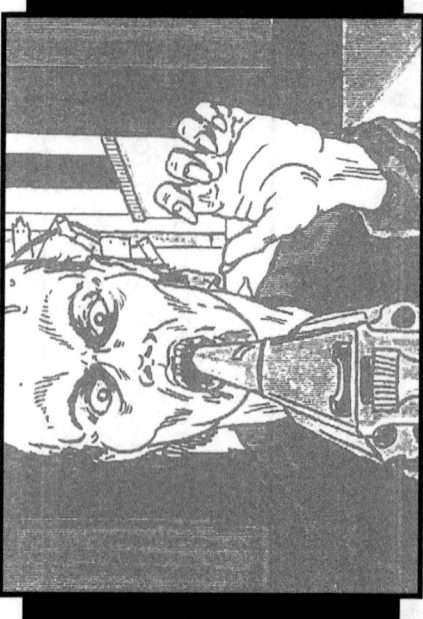
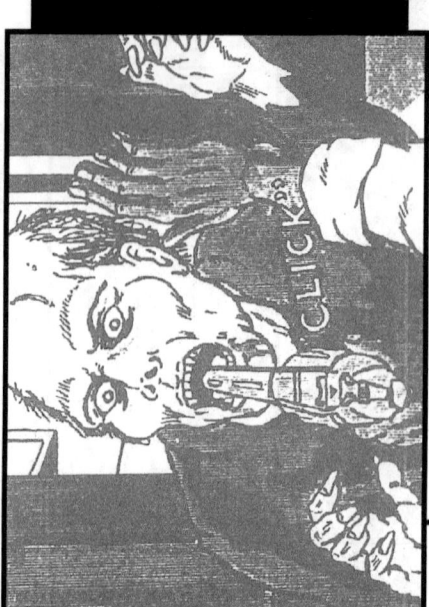

I wanted him to put the gun barrel into the zombie's mouth and start pulling the trigger. Sort of a "zombie roulette" as we see the bullet getting closer to the firing hammer.

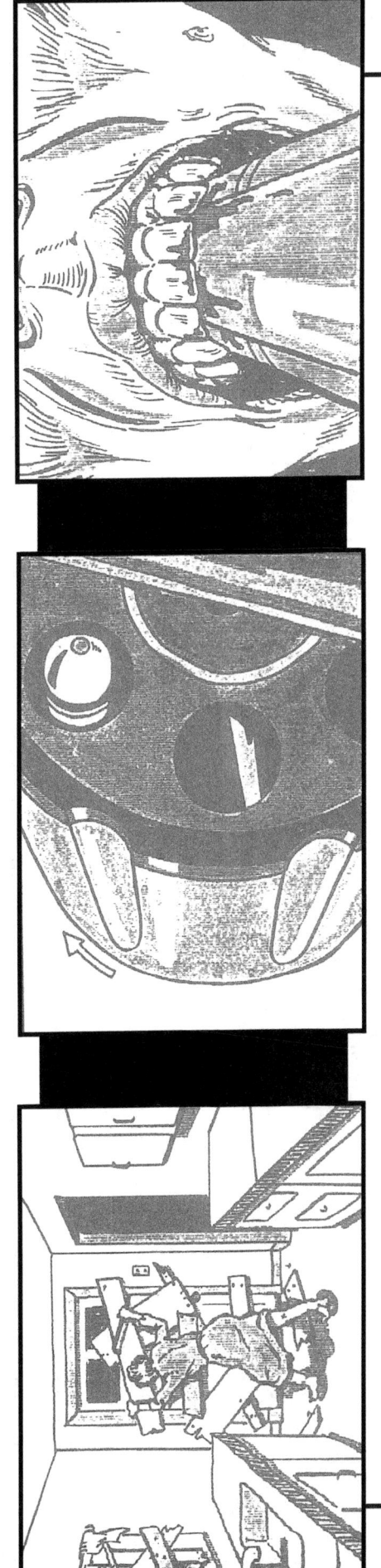

Meanwhile Barbara is in danger—but Ben has to deal with this zombie and pulling the trigger... hoping.

The gun finally fires and I was going to do a "James Cameron white frame" and become the bullet passing through flesh and brain....

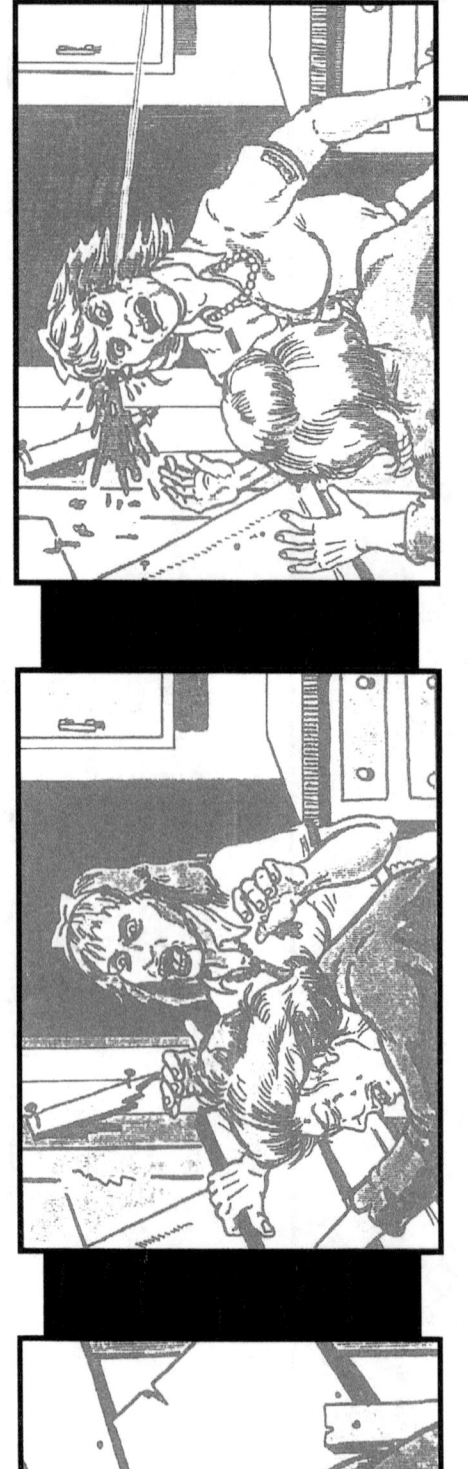

...until the same bullet kills the zombie attacking Barbara. SHOT DOWN. "There's no time for all that." This time my effects team was in on it. They didn't bother building the flesh frames that I could use to shoot the bullet traveling to the zombie.

Barbara leaves because, "You can outrun these things," and see zombies chewing on the charred remains of Tom and Judy.

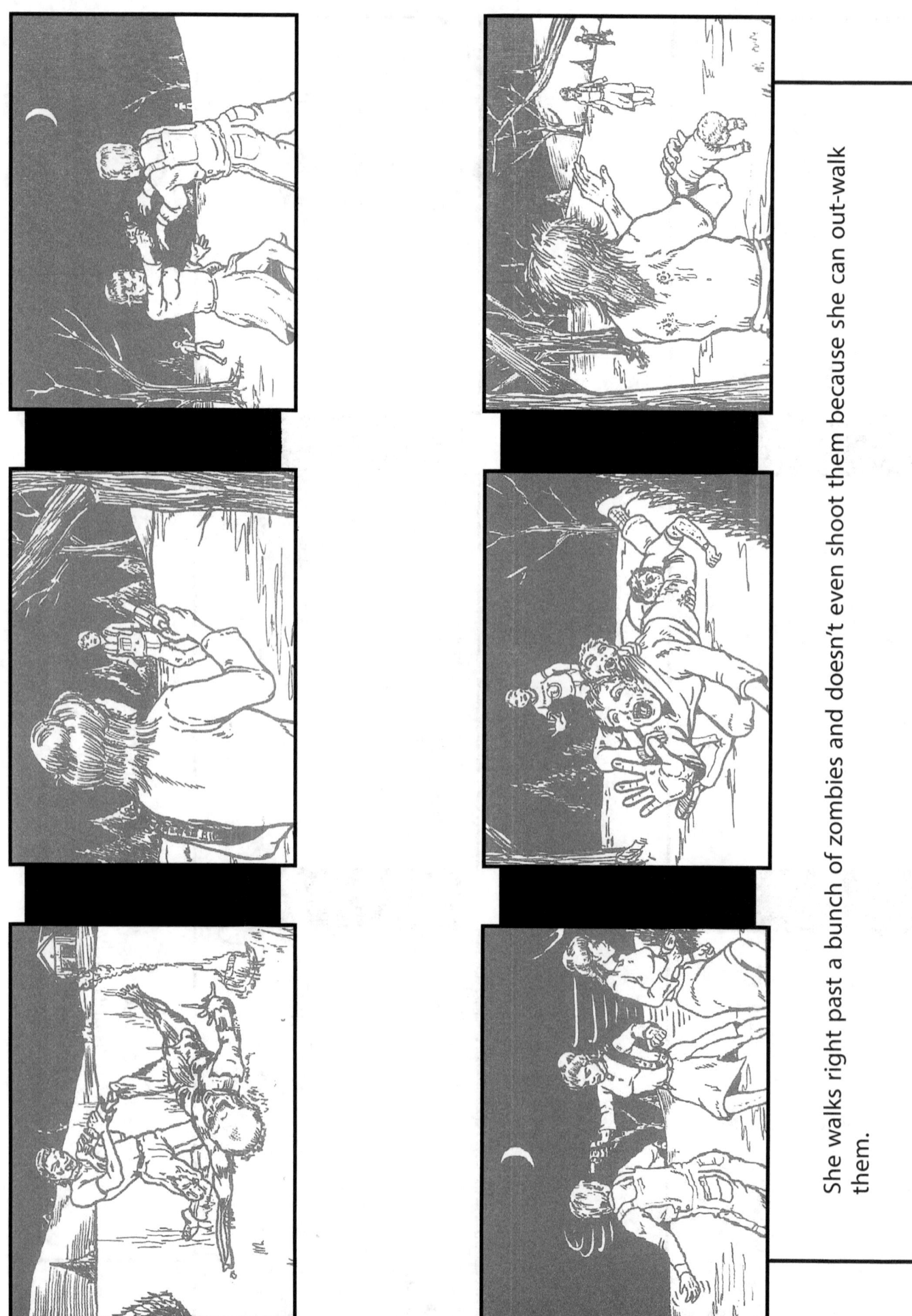

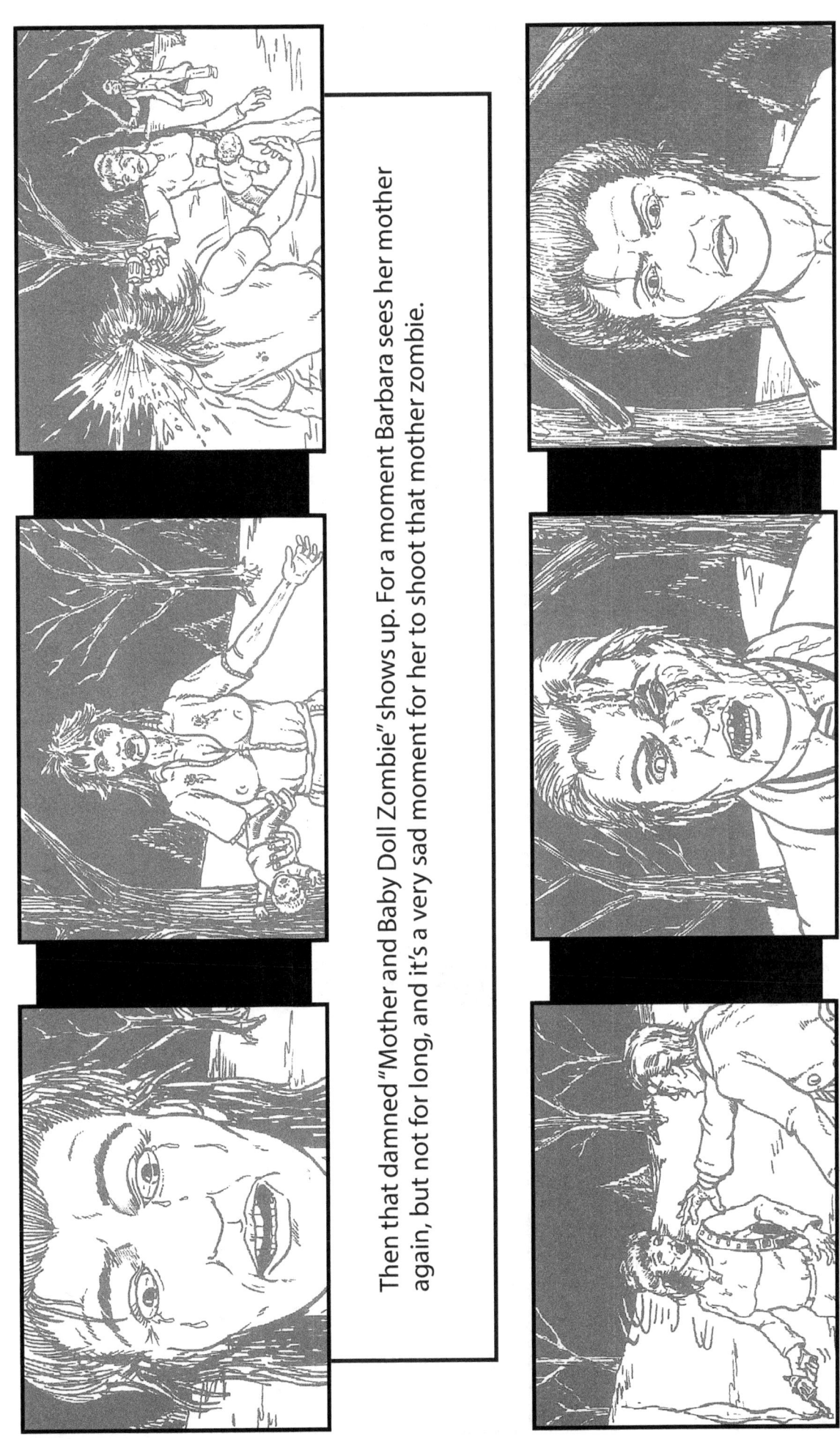

Then that damned "Mother and Baby Doll Zombie" shows up. For a moment Barbara sees her mother again, but not for long, and it's a very sad moment for her to shoot that mother zombie.

All of a sudden Johnny shows up, zombified. Barbara is getting a little shell-shocked—and without hesitation blasts him away.

Ben is still looking for the keys, and suddenly the Helen zombie surfaces. I thought he should blast her away—just as she died at the hands of her daughter—in shadow. She dies finally again in shadow.

Ben finds the gas keys and this is just hilarious to him after all they've been through. If only he had gone down to the basement. Get it?

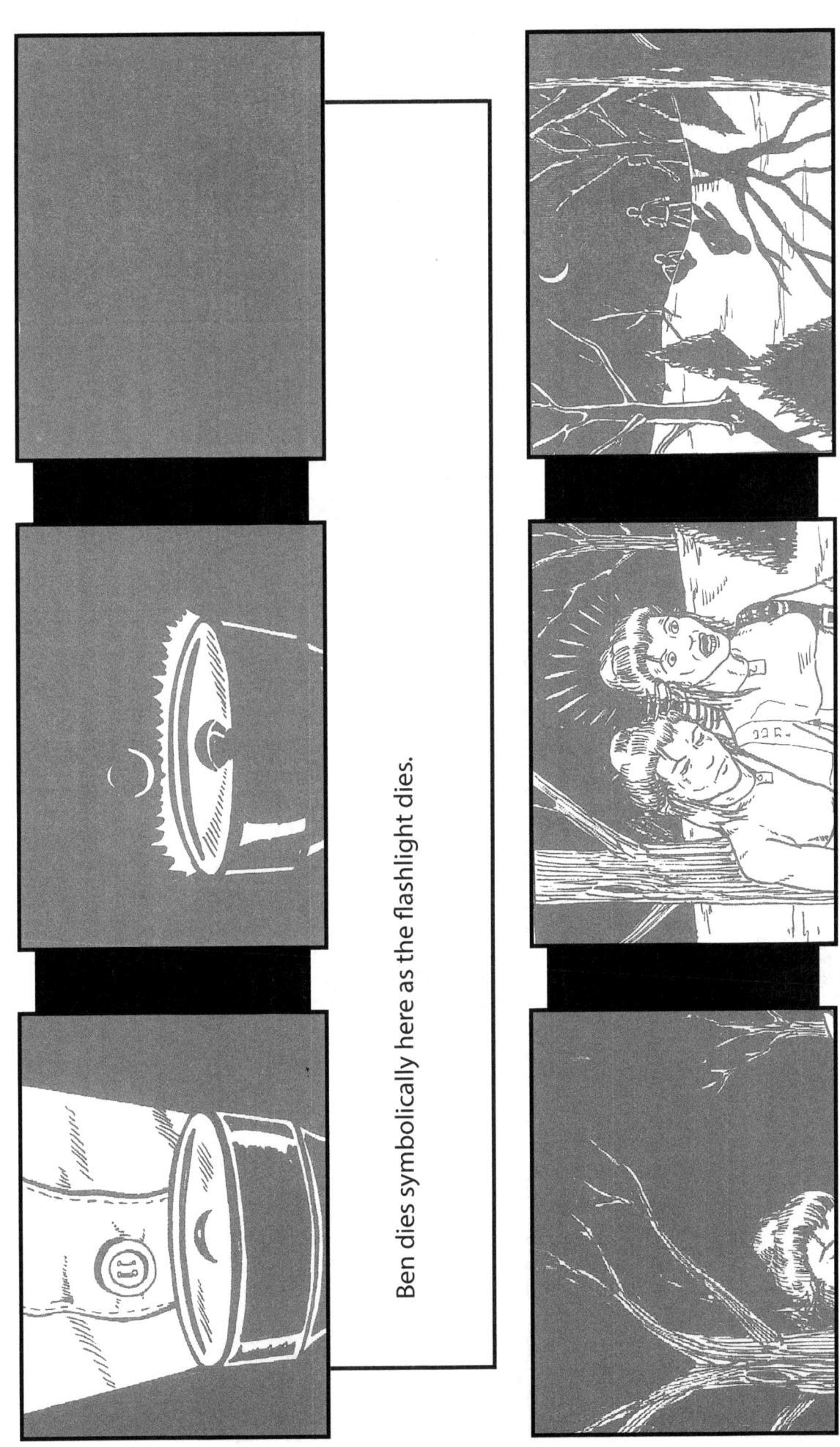

Barbara is shot at by the rednecks who think she is a zombie.

Barbara wakes up and sees the rednecks are just having a good old time, making a carnival out of shooting the zombies.

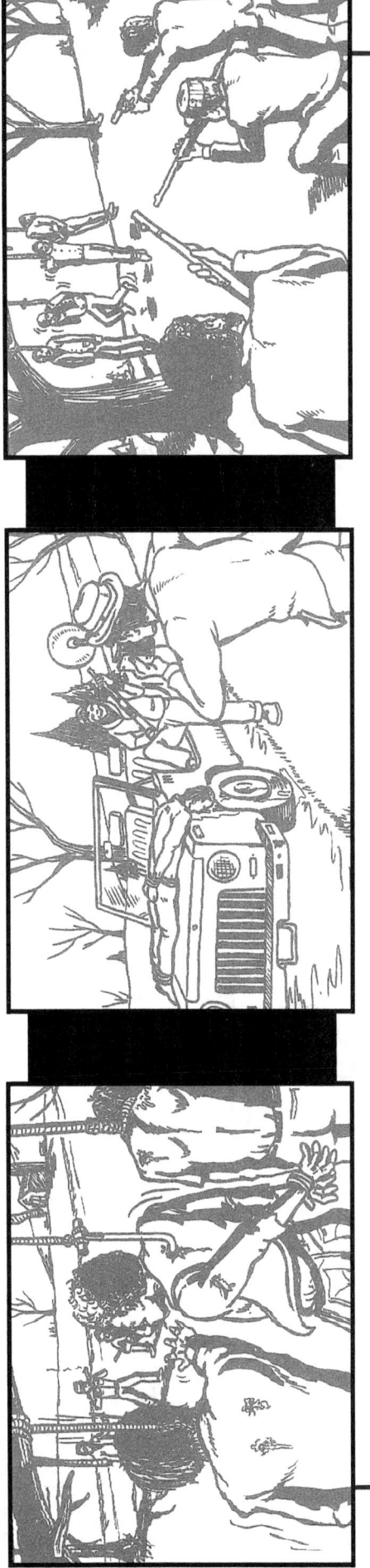

I wanted to establish a photographer wandering around the group so the still photos at the end, like the original, made sense. You know, just in case we did the ending in my version.

THESE ARE NOW THE DRAMATIC LAST BITS OF *THE VERSION YOU'VE NEVER SEEN BEFORE.*

Barbara heads back to the house and thinks she sees Ben moving around in the attic.

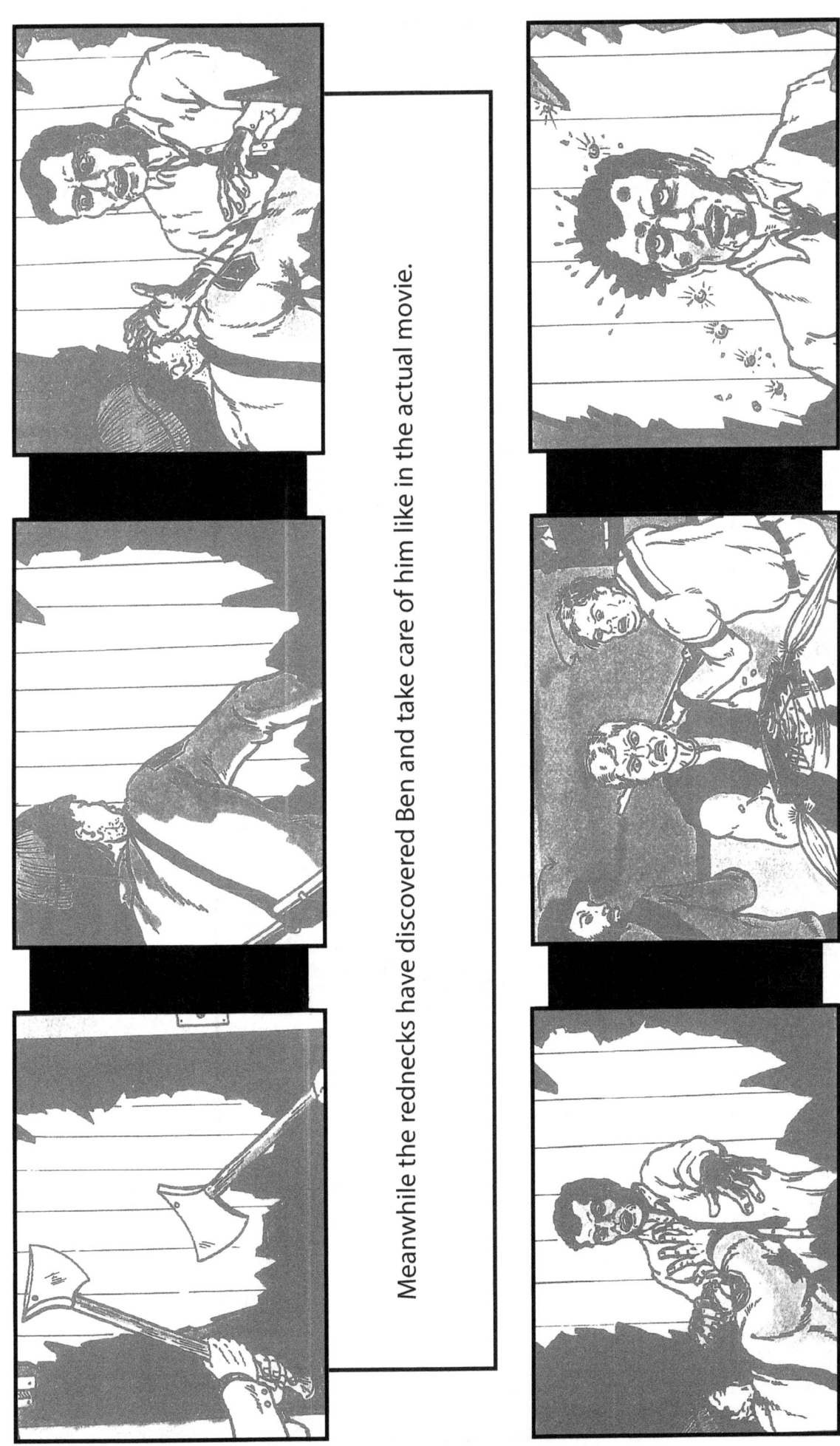

BUT...

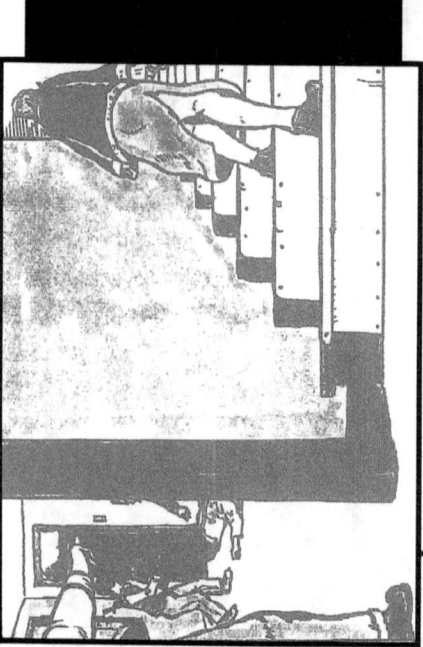

Barbara goes into the house straight up to the attic.

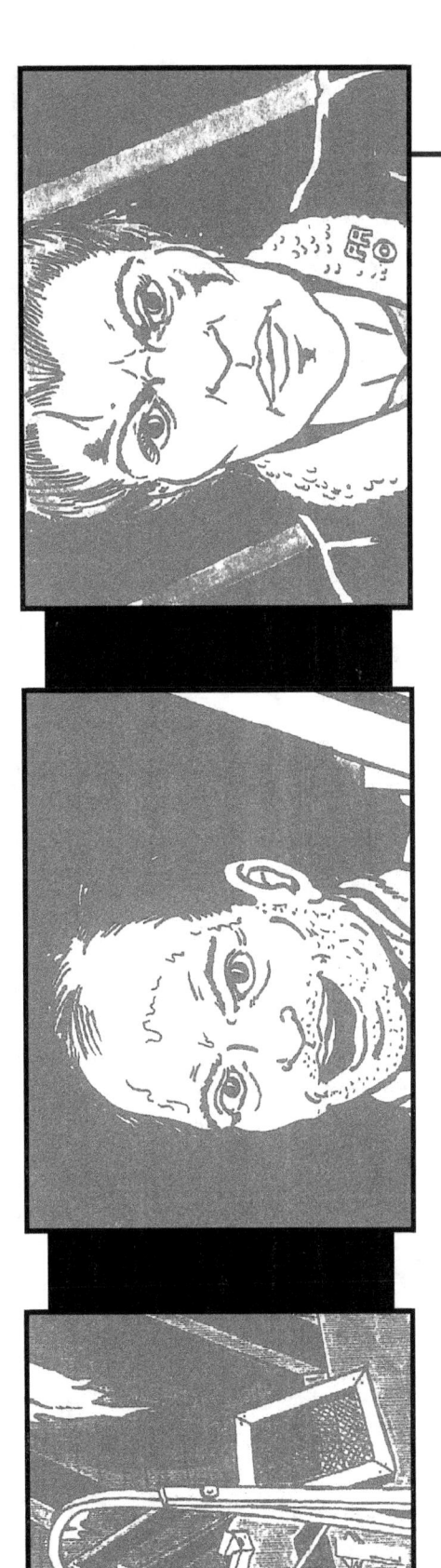

The attic is full of junk and in one corner is a full-length mirror. Harry peeks out from behind the mirror says his line here, "You came back…"

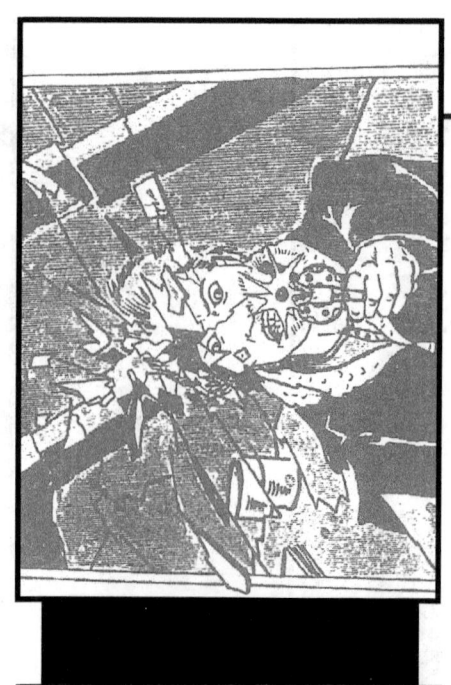

...and a two-shot is created of Harry and Barbara. Barbara only in the mirror. Harry retreats behind the mirror and...

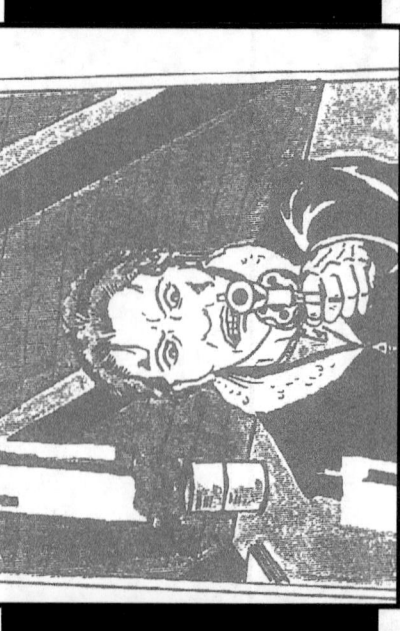

...we see Barbara raise the gun and she fires. The mirror and her image shatters. If you've seen Kubrick's *Lolita*, this was an homage.

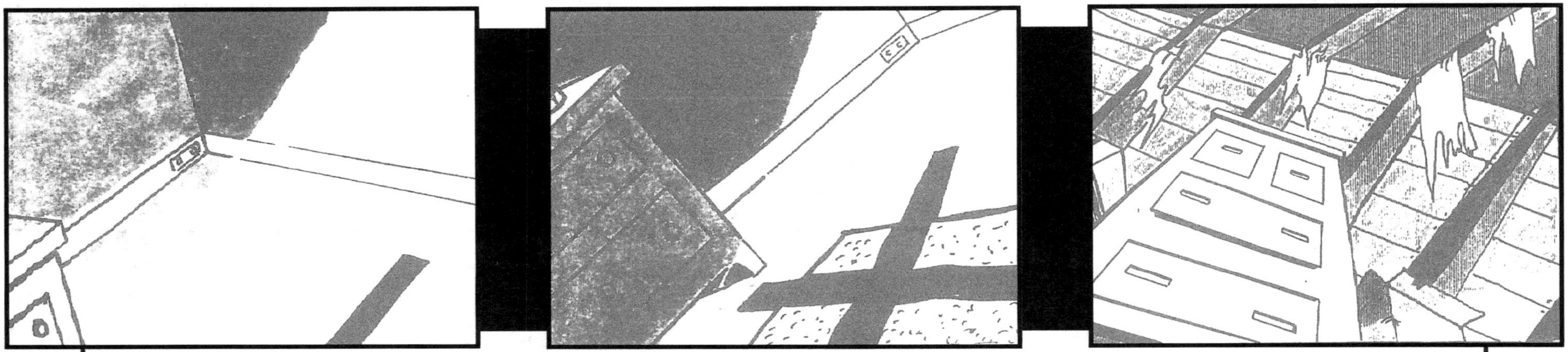

We now see Harry's point of view as he falls to the floor.

The last thing he sees is Barbara's distorted image in the broken glass of the mirror.

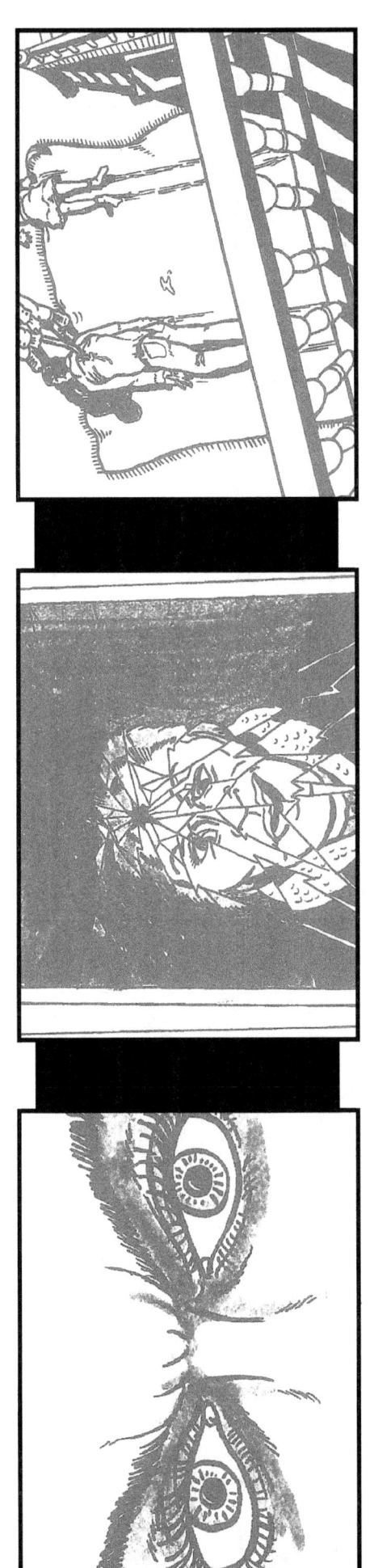

This is when Barbara becomes one of them. "They are us, we are them," because she just killed Harry in cold blood. She yells down to the rednecks that, "There's another one for the fire up here," as she watches them drag Ben out.

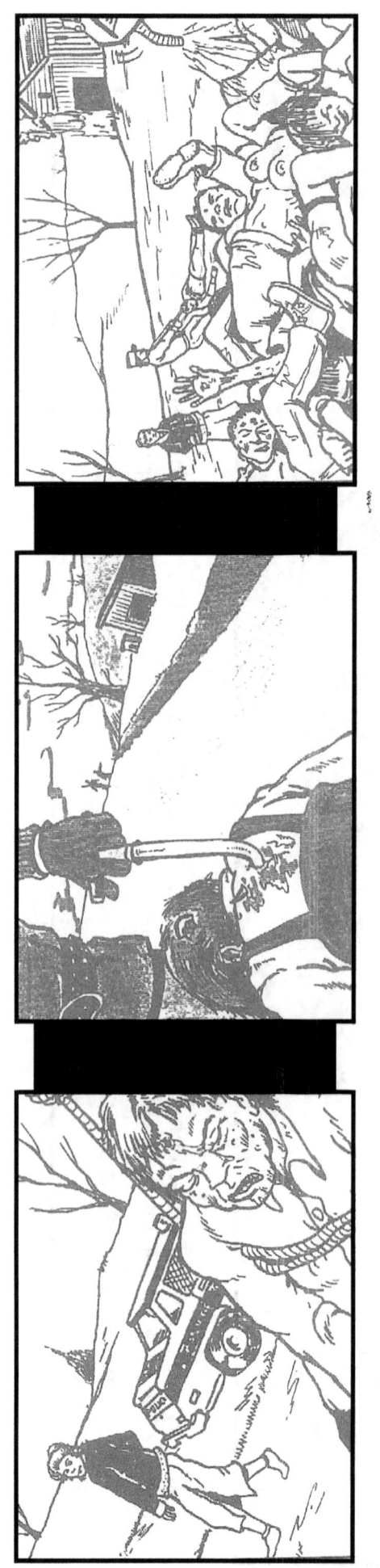

Some still images and Barbara sees them drag Ben and Harry to the fire.

The end credits would happen over seeing Ben and Harry burn to nothing, face-to-face, and a close up of Barbara's eyes.

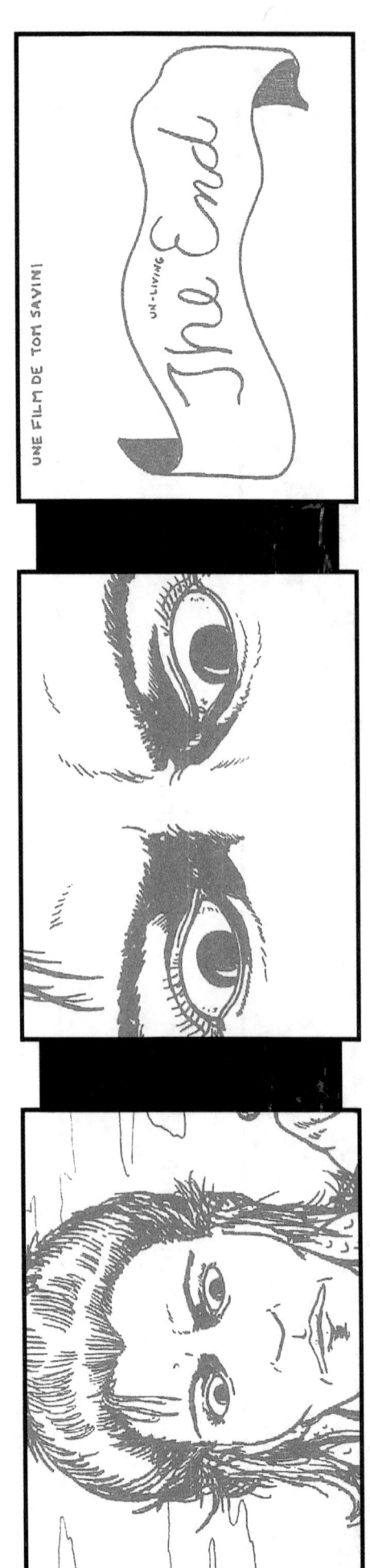

GALLERY

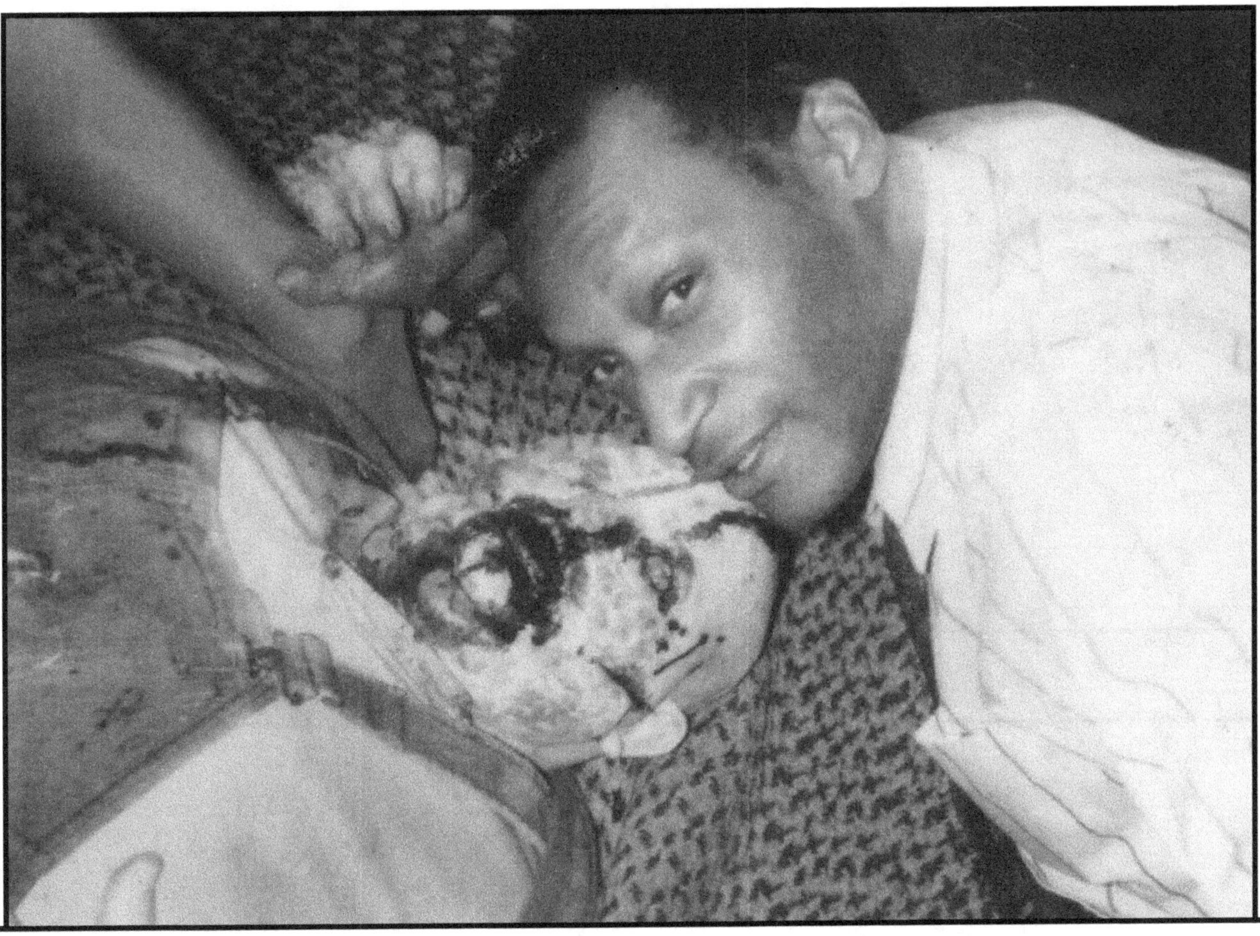

Tony Todd and Pat Logan.

Bills dummy for the tombstone hit.

Bill Moseley and his Dummy (created by John Vulich and Everett Burrell).

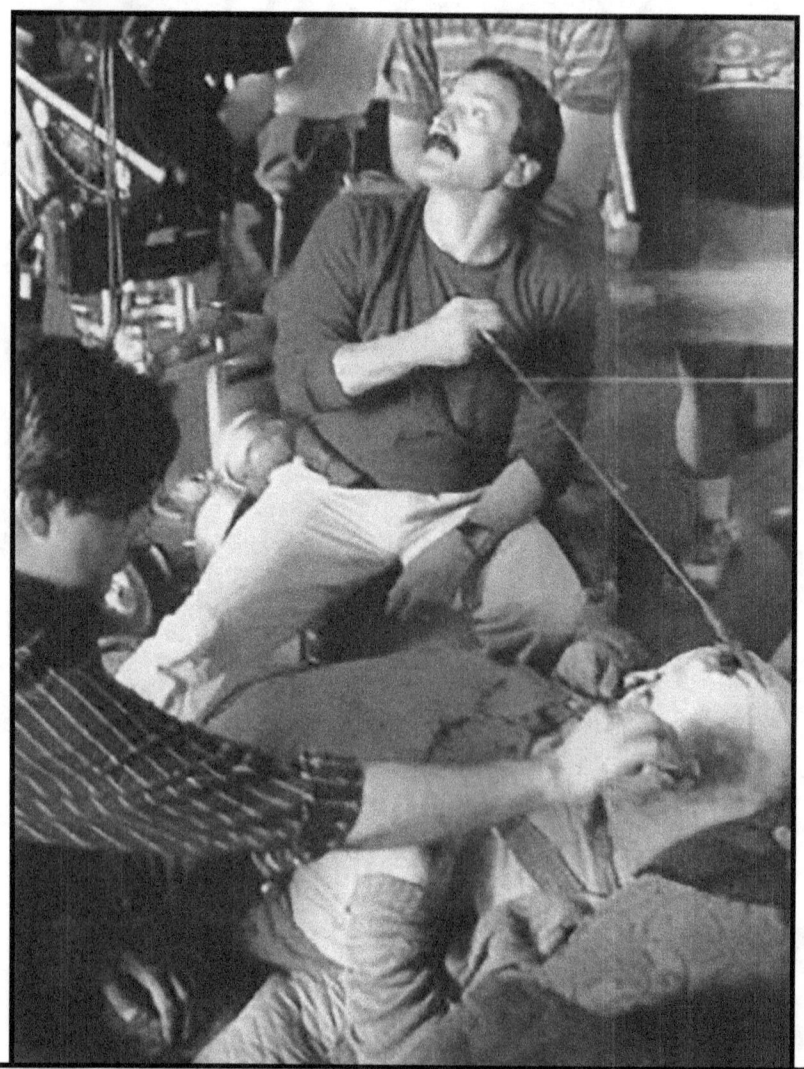

I was showing the camera how I wanted the poker to pull against Pat's wound.

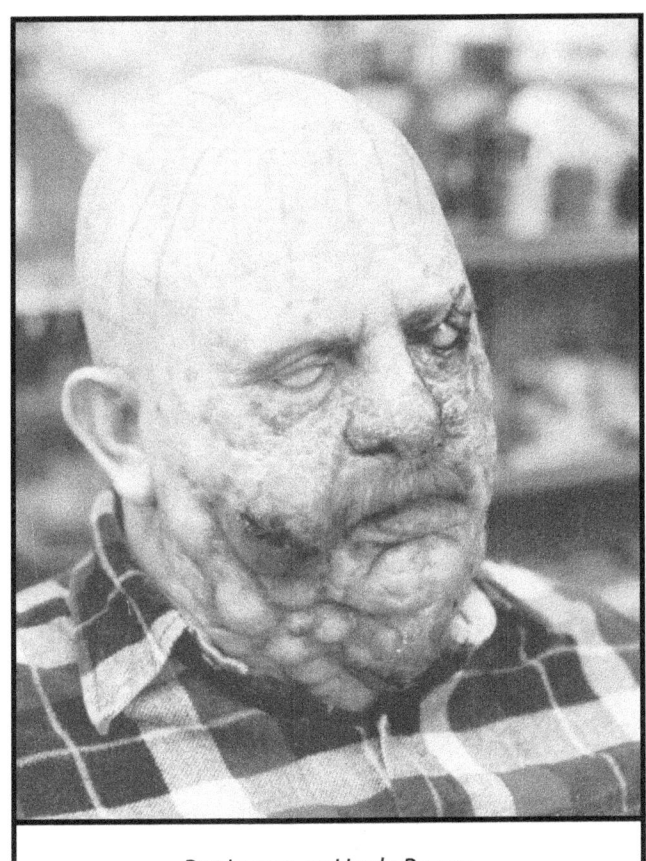

Pat Logan as Uncle Reege.

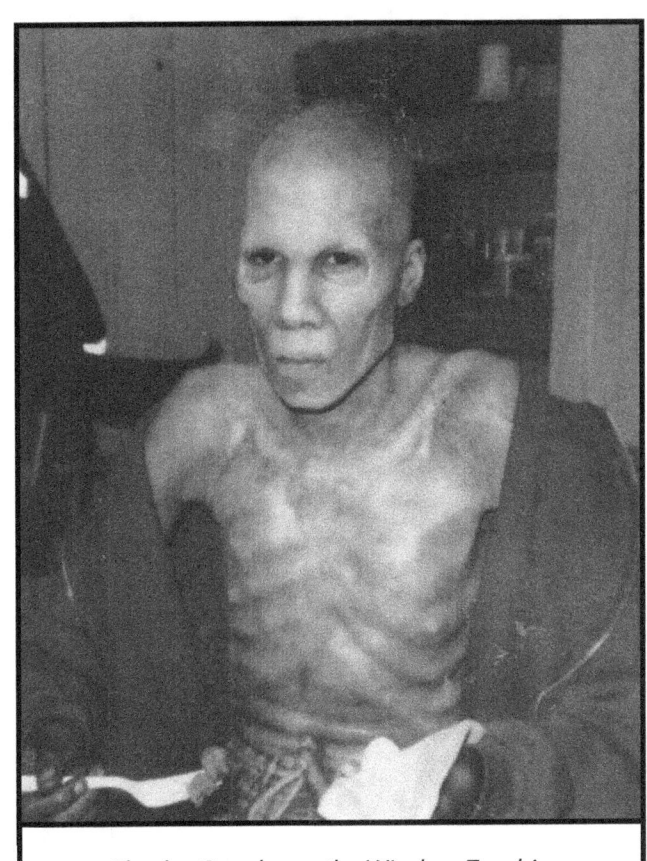

Charles Crawley as the Window Zombie.

Dyrk Ashton as the Truck Zombie.

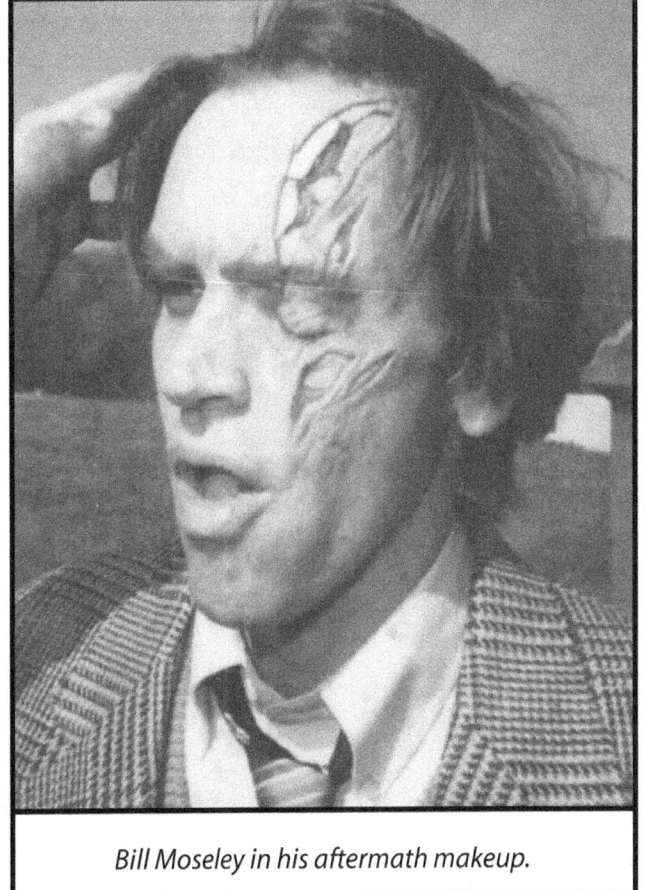

Bill Moseley in his aftermath makeup.

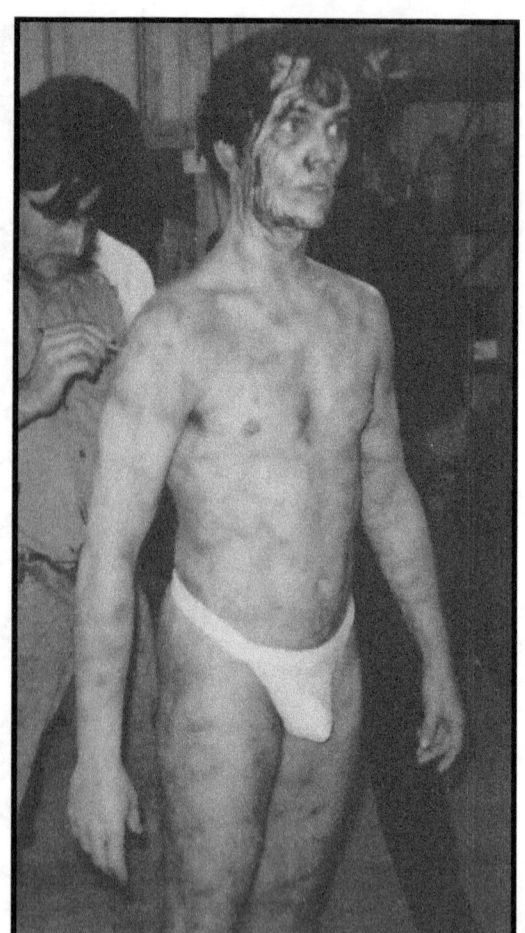 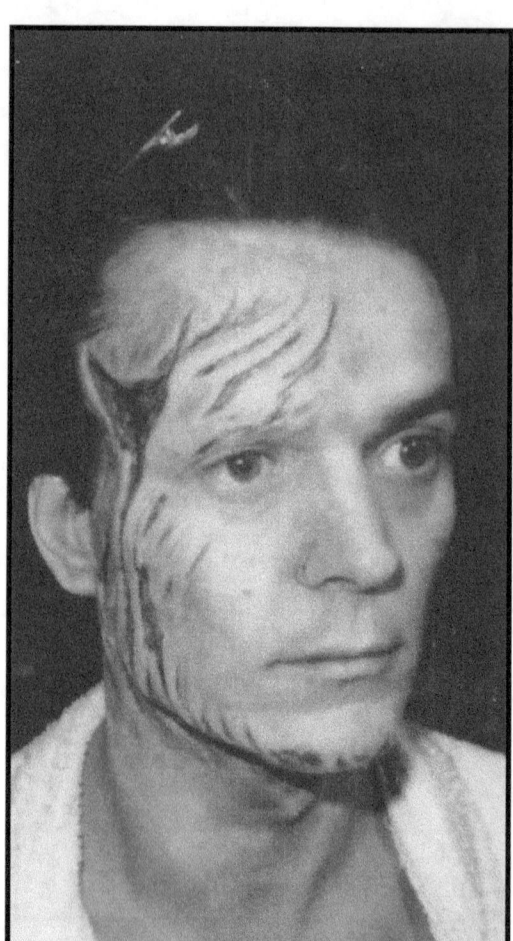

Another zombie make up.

A test of the "Truck Zombie" twisted rig on JJ, one of the crew guys.

Patty with a zombie extra and my daughter, Lia.

Me with Mr. Magruder zombie.

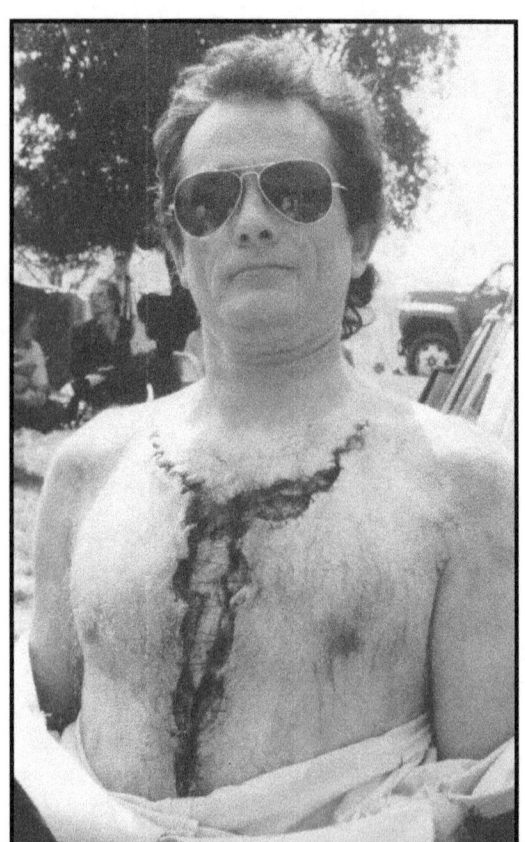

Tim Carrier, The Autopsy Zombie and movement instructor.

John Vulich with Tim Carrier.

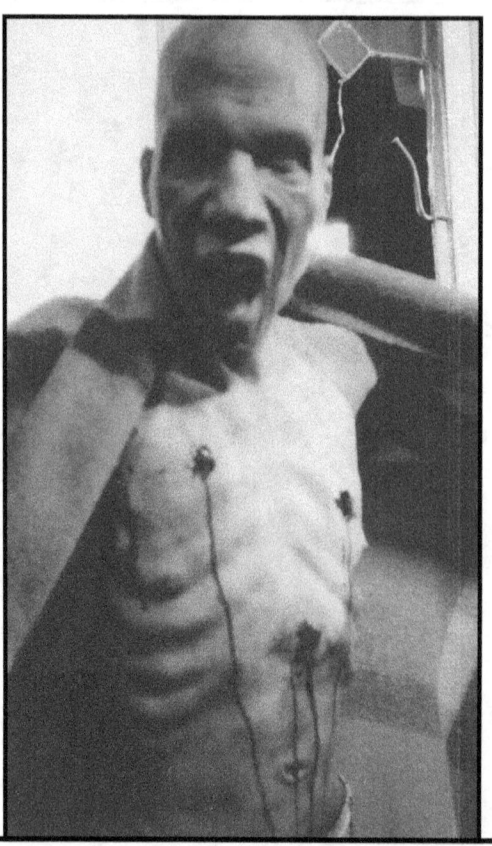

Charles Crawley as the Window Zombie.

L-R: Director Tom Savini, Tom Towles (Harry Cooper), Patricia Tallman (Barbara), Jeannee Josefczyk (Make-up artist).

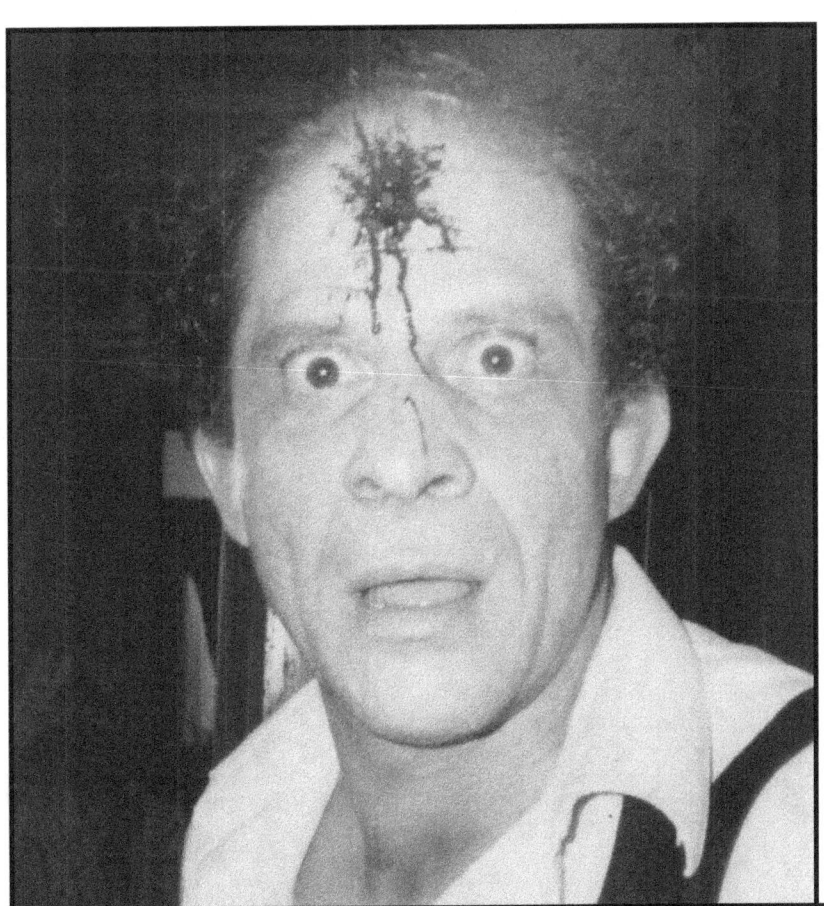

We used breakaway glass balls filled with blood to fire at actors foreheads for the head hits, like this one on Tom Towles.

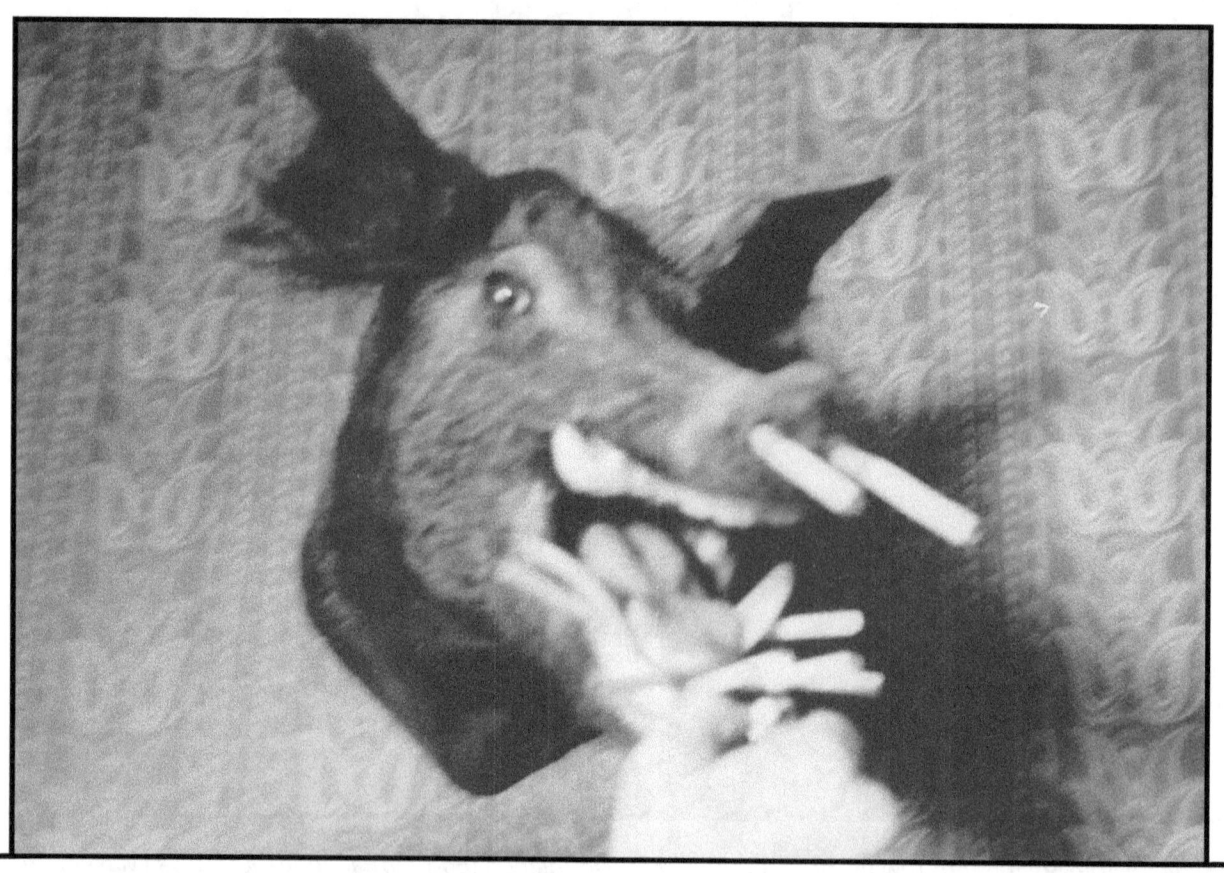

One day we stuffed cigarettes into the animal on the wall.

Patty with Art Director Cletus Anderson.

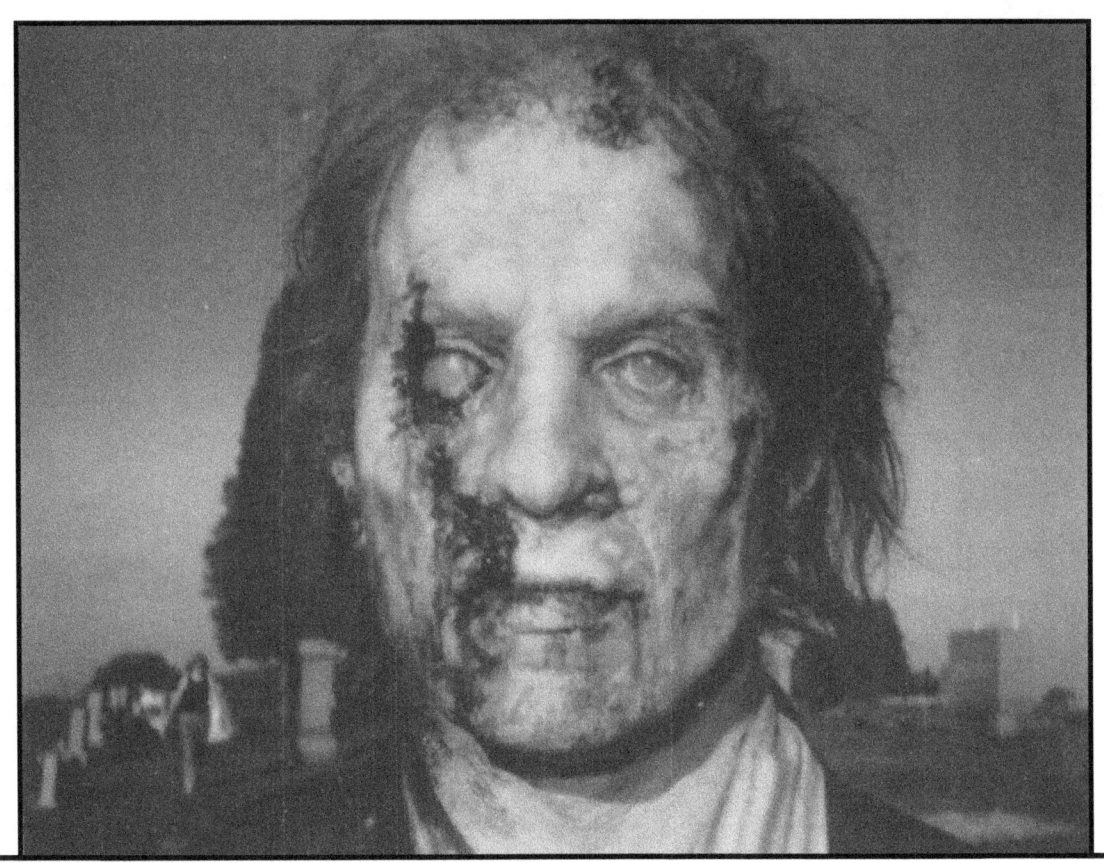

Greg Funk as the Cemetery Zombie.

This is a photo I got from Patty after I called and asked her to be in the film.

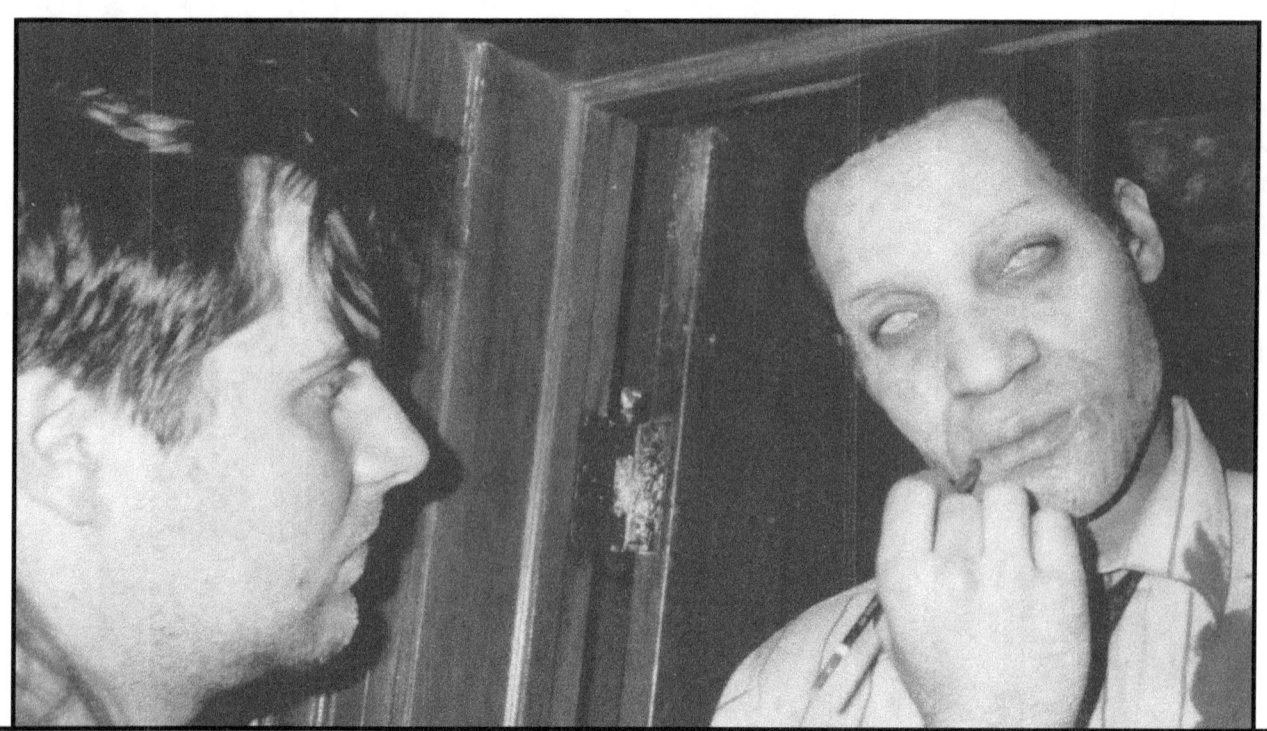

John Vulich and Tony Todd.

A backstage group shot.

Pat Reese, the first "maybe a zombie" in the cemetery. A fine actor from my theatre days.

Russ Streiner as the Sheriff, with the rednecks and corpse pile.

Some of the last frames I shot for the photo ending.

Me in the "Animal Room," contemplating my next move.

www.ingramcontent.com/pod-product-compliance
Lightning Source LLC
Chambersburg PA
CBHW082044250426
43661CB00080B/2776